FERNS

FERNS

INDOORS
OUTDOORS
GROWING
CRAFTING

Mobee Weinstein

COOL
SPRINGS
PRESS

Inspiring | Educating | Creating | Entertaining

Brimming with creative inspiration, how-to projects, and useful information to enrich your everyday life, Quarto Knows is a favorite destination for those pursuing their interests and passions. Visit our site and dig deeper with our books into your area of interest: Quarto Creates, Quarto Cooks, Quarto Homes, Quarto Lives, Quarto Drives, Quarto Explores, Quarto Gifts, or Quarto Kids.

First Published in 2020 by Cool Springs Press, an imprint of The Quarto Group,
100 Cummings Center, Suite 265-D, Beverly, MA 01915, USA.
T (978) 282-9590 F (978) 283-2742
QuartoKnows.com

Cool Springs Press titles are also available at discount for retail, wholesale, promotional, and bulk purchase. For details, contact the Special Sales Manager by email at specialsales@quarto.com or by mail at The Quarto Group, Attn: Special Sales Manager, 100 Cummings Center, Suite 265-D, Beverly, MA 01915, USA.

24 23 22 21 20   1 2 3 4 5

ISBN: 978-0-7603-6898-5

Digital edition published in 2020
eISBN: 978-0-7603-6395-9

Library of Congress Cataloging-in-Publication Data
Names: Weinstein, Mobee, author.
Title: The complete book of ferns : indoors — outdoors — growing — crafting — history & lore / Mobee Weinstein.
Description: Beverly, Massachusetts : Cool Springs Press, 2019. | Includes index.
Identifiers: LCCN 2019032527 (print) | LCCN 2019032528 (ebook) | ISBN 9780760363942 (hardback) | ISBN 9780760363959 (ebook)
Subjects: LCSH: Ferns.
Classification: LCC QK522 .W45 2019 (print) | LCC QK522 (ebook) | DDC 587/.3—dc23
LC record available at https://lccn.loc.gov/2019032527
LC ebook record available at https://lccn.loc.gov/2019032528

Design and page layout: Laura Shaw Design, Inc.
Printed in China

DEDICATED TO MY MOTHER,
SUE CLARK

CONTENTS

| CHAPTER 1 |

HISTORY AND USES

ALTHOUGH FERNS MAY seem simple and unassuming, especially when compared to the blooms of showy flowering plants such as colorful hibiscus or fragrant roses, they are among the world's greatest evolutionary success stories. Ferns have been part of the Earth's many ecosystems for hundreds of millions of years. You may find it hard to believe, but that small, feathery fern tucked in the corner of your garden, and the potted fern sitting on your bookshelf, are anything but simple. Ferns are tough, complex characters. Through changing climates, moving continents, and mass extinctions, ferns have carried on steadily and mostly unfazed. It's no wonder they've been used and appreciated by humans throughout our shared history. And it's no wonder that we humans continue to cultivate and adore ferns. Today, ferns are in the midst of a modern renaissance. Thanks to the continued rise in the popularity of houseplants, coupled with the

adaptability, diversity, and aesthetics of ferns, this amazing group of plants graces our homes and gardens with greenery and texture, and will no doubt continue to do so for generations to come.

Let's start by taking an in-depth look at the evolutionary history of ferns and learning why they are such successful plants. Then, we'll examine the inner workings of their life cycles, their myriad of forms, growth habits, and favored growing climates, and information on how to propagate these unique plants. In Chapters 3 and 4, you'll discover profiles of more than 70 popular indoor and outdoor fern species, and care information to cultivate these plants in your home or landscape. The final chapter is dedicated to creative planting projects for growing ferns in some pretty surprising and inspired ways, along with a handful of techniques for turning ferns into works of art you can proudly display in your home.

Understanding how ferns came to be and the role these plants played in the evolution of the Earth we know today is the first step on our fern journey.

The Evolution of Ferns

You might be tempted to think ferns are primitive simply because they've been around for so long, and they may at first seem unremarkable. But ferns are prime examples of finding a winning formula and sticking with it. The interrupted fern, *Claytosmunda claytoniana* (syn. *Osmunda claytoniana*), for example, which is currently part of the native flora in eastern Asia and eastern North America and is at home in gardens as well as wild spaces, is a textbook illustration. Fossils of this exact fern have been found to be at least 180 million years old. By every measure, right down to the level of the fossilized cells, the modern interrupted fern appears to be totally unchanged after all those eons. Not only would this fern have been just as familiar to *Tyrannosaurus rex* as it is to us, but it had been growing happily for more than 100 million years before *T. rex* even appeared on the scene.

The history of evolving plant life has been marked by several important changes. Ferns are in a group of plants known as the seedless vascular plants, meaning they have one of the biggest innovations of plant life (vascular tissue), but lack another (flowers and seeds).

Claytosmunda claytoniana (syn. *Osmunda claytoniana*), the interrupted fern, has remained unchanged for 180 million years.

To understand how ferns evolved, we first have to look at how the simplest of plants came to be and how those plants went on to change and evolve.

SIMPLE ORGANISMS

Some of the simpler organisms are the single-celled green algae, which generally make their living floating in water and photosynthesizing. Eventually, those single cells began to form larger, multi-celled organisms often called seaweed. Algae were likely the first land inhabitants living in a wet film and they are believed to have given rise to the increasingly more complex earliest land plants, liverworts and mosses. These are the earlier, nonvascular plants, which means they lack a vascular system to move water from one part of the plant to another. For algae living in the water, this is obviously not a problem, but for nonvascular plants on the land, such as mosses, the lack of a vascular system significantly restricts the size of the plant. Mosses can soak up water like a sponge, but their lack of a system to pump water up from the ground means they can't support tall stems or wide leaves. As a result, mosses remain low, ground-hugging cushions.

▼ Tall vascular plants and the first ferns began to inhabit the Earth hundreds of millions of years ago.

VASCULAR PLANTS

Plant life started to rise off the ground when the first vascular plants arrived on the scene some 425 million years ago. Vascular tissue, which consists of tiny tubes running up plant stems, sometimes further strengthened with the organic compound lignin, freed plants from clinging to the ground. Being tall is no great virtue on its own, but when a plant is fighting with other plants for valuable sunlight, height allows it to shade out the competition. Nonvascular plants, which had been happily forming green carpets basking in the sun, suddenly had to adjust to living in the deep shade of their taller competitors, or extreme

conditions in which their tall relatives couldn't survive. Mosses, liverworts, and their kin got pushed to the sidelines over the next several million years as vascular plants quickly dominated the surface of the Earth, towering 100 to 150 feet (30.5 to 46 m) in the air. It is at this time that the first ferns made their appearance.

This explosion of lignin-reinforced vascular tubes enabled plants to reach soaring heights, creating the first forests. These massive forests in turn created an important facet of our modern world: coal. The era of seedless forests was also a time of very active plate tectonics. Continents were crashing into each other, pushing up mountain ranges and burying some of those new forests deep underground, transforming their trunks and foliage into the coal that fueled the Industrial Revolution.

SEED PLANTS

The next big evolutionary change in plants left ferns behind. The first seed plants arrived on the scene some 350 million years ago. Ferns and other seedless plants such as mosses reproduce via spores (more about this reproductive strategy in Chapter 2). Each tiny spore is fragile, requiring constant moisture to germinate and produce another

▶ Most ferns survive under the canopy of larger trees thanks to a special gene for a light-sensing protein called neochrome, which allows the plant to respond to the presence of red light.

generation of ferns. Seeds, on the other hand, give a baby plant a start-up package. Inside each seed is an embryo and, almost always, a supply of food; when a seed germinates, it has time to develop an initial root to harvest water before it begins to photosynthesize. This technique of giving baby plants a head start in life was wildly successful and allowed forests of conifers to dominate the landscape.

The Many Uses of Ferns

Ferns have been put to many uses by humans over our long history. We've been eating ferns for a long time, and many cultures around the world eat a wide variety of fern species, mostly harvesting the new fronds before they've fully unfolded, at the so-called "fiddlehead" stage. Bracken ferns are of course eaten this way, but quite a few other species are as well. In Taiwan and elsewhere in Asia, the fronds of the bird's nest fern (the genus *Asplenium*) are popular as a vegetable. These tropical ferns are popular as houseplants around the world, and their broad, leafy fronds are quite tasty as well.

Unfortunately, there is mounting evidence that many ferns, not just bracken

◀ Fiddleheads are a springtime delicacy in many parts of the world.

fern, are possibly carcinogenic if eaten regularly, despite being tasty. If you want to indulge in fiddleheads, it is best to do so in moderation.

The stems of the *Equisetum* species, commonly called scouring rush or horsetail, contain silica and can be used to scour pots and pans. They can also be used to file wood and to make reeds for clarinets.

One type of aquatic fern, the genus *Azolla*, is an effective fertilizer. This tiny fern has a symbiotic relationship with a cyanobacterium that converts nitrogen in the atmosphere into a form that plants can use as fertilizer. Because *Azolla*, when partnered with its bacterial friend, can produce its own fertilizer, this little fern can become a pest, doubling its mass every few days and quickly covering large water surfaces. But the vigor of *Azolla* has been put to good use in Asian rice farming. Rice needs a lot of nitrogen to produce maximum yields, so farmers inoculate rice paddies with *Azolla*, encouraging it to spread rapidly and release its nitrogen bounty to the rice as it decomposes.

Azolla is attracting new attention from researchers, in part because of this humble little fern's history. Around 50 million years ago, the world was a very different place, and much warmer thanks to high levels of greenhouse gases in the atmosphere. The Arctic Ocean was essentially a huge, warm lake—the perfect habitat for *Azolla* ferns. It was so

perfect that *Azolla* formed thick mats, covering the surface of the water. *Azolla* ferns periodically died and sank below the surface, only to be replaced by new mats of this rapidly growing fern. This cycle continued for roughly a million years. When the *Azolla* sank, it took with it the carbon it had taken from the air to fuel photosynthesis. Over a million years, this amounted to an enormous quantity of carbon, enough so that the amount of carbon dioxide in the air was cut to about half what it had been before the age of *Azolla* began. The changes in Earth's climate are incredibly complex, but it is thought that this fern may have been part of why Earth shifted to a cooler climate cycle, leading to ice ages and eventually the climate we are familiar with today.

Although we might not be able to use massive amounts of *Azolla* to suck carbon directly out of the air to fight climate change today (and we don't have a million years to wait) researchers are finding new uses for this simple fern that might help us reduce our carbon footprint and live more lightly. In addition to its long history of use as a natural fertilizer, *Azolla* is now being used to filter and clean gray water. This little fern is also edible and highly nutritious, and its prodigious growth rate means that, with minimal inputs, it could become an easy food source for livestock.

Finally, ferns are, of course, used for their aesthetics. It's plain and simple— people like looking at ferns. Their intricate fronds, divided into smaller leaflets in a kind of fractal geometry, are beautiful examples of complex designs created from simple rules. The airy, lacy texture of many ferns evokes delicacy and fragility, but ferns are astonishingly tough, preceding and outlasting the reign of dinosaurs and the arrival and end of ice ages. Surely they'll outlast us as well.

We visit museums and travel to historic sites to view snippets of our own tiny place in Earth's history. When we plant ferns in the garden or in containers indoors, we get to live with some of the oldest organisms on the planet. Maybe if we all spent more time with ferns, we'd learn something of their secret to living with grace, beauty, and strength.

◄ *Azolla* is a water-dwelling, floating fern that once formed thick mats over parts of Earth's oceans. As layers of *Azolla* settled to the bottom, it captured carbon and may have helped change Earth's climate.

CHAPTER 2

THE BOTANY OF FERNS

OFTEN PEOPLE "identify" a plant as a fern simply based on the appearance of delicate, lacy leaves. Although this may be characteristic of many ferns, it isn't the case for all, and its not a sufficient way to identify them. Some plants have a fernlike appearance but are not ferns. The asparagus fern, named partly for its fernlike looks, is a perfect example. It isn't an actual fern but rather an asparagus. And although it's related to the food that shares the first half of its common name, the asparagus fern is not edible either. Ferns have familiar plant parts (roots, stems, and leaves) and the ferns we all instantly recognize have lacy foliage, but they're quite diverse in their appearance. What all ferns have in common, however, is the fact that they do not make flowers, fruit, or seed. If you see a plant with a flower, fruit, or seed, you're not looking at a fern!

So how can you know whether a particular plant is a fern? And what,

exactly, is a fern? Botanically speaking, a fern is "a vascular plant with megaphylls that reproduces by spore." Unless you've studied some botany, that definition is probably too technical to be helpful. To understand what makes a fern a fern, let's start by looking at the three terms mentioned in that botanical definition: *vascular*, *megaphyll*, and *spore*.

WHAT IS A VASCULAR PLANT?

A vascular plant is one that has a specialized internal system for transporting water, minerals, and food throughout the plant. Think of it as a kind of plumbing system. Most of the obvious and familiar plants found on Earth today are vascular plants. In addition to the ferns, all seed-producing plants share this trait. Seed-producing plants include all flowering plants, as well as conifers (cone-bearing plants such as pines, firs, spruces, and all their varied relatives).

With rare exceptions, vascular plants are comprised of distinct parts: roots, stems, and leaves. In contrast, examples of non-vascular plants include the mosses.

WHAT IS A MEGAPHYLL?

Megaphyll is the botanical term for a type of leaf. Literally, it translates to "large leaf," but it's defined as a complex leaf with branching veins. Such leaves are not strangers to you. Even if you're not familiar with a particular fern leaf, when you look at the leaves of seed-producing plants, you're also looking at megaphylls. Just a few examples are the leaves of maple, oak, and pine trees, petunias, sunflowers, corn, and rice. While ferns have megaphylls, other similar-looking plants called lycophytes differ in that they have microphylls (see sidebar for more on fern allies). A microphyll ("small leaf") is simply a leaf with a single, unbranched vein. As their name implies, having a single, nonbranching vein greatly limits their size. So the broad, lacy leaves of a fern are megaphylls, while the narrow, almost scale-like leaves of clubmosses and spikemosses are microphylls.

SEED PLANTS
ANGIOSPERMS AND GYMNOSPERMS

Angiosperm and *gymnosperm* are terms used to describe the two basic groups of seed-producing plants.

➤ The **angiosperms** are commonly known as the flowering plants. Their flowers develop into fruits that contain seeds. Angiosperms are the most diverse and dominant group of plants on Earth today. Roses, water lilies, tulips, sunflowers, apples, and magnolias are but a few examples.

➤ The **gymnosperms** do not make flowers and therefore do not make fruit. Instead, their seeds rest on "naked" leaves, or scales, which are more typically clustered into cones. Gymnosperms, the oldest of the living seed plants, most likely came from ancient "seed ferns" and are probably the ancestors of modern flowering plants. Conifers such as pine, spruce, cypress, and redwood are examples of gymnosperms. Cycads, which are better known in tropical and subtropical climates, and the well-known ginkgo tree are also examples of gymnosperms. Another member of this group, *Ephedra*, is known for treating breathing problems (it's an ingredient in the medication Sudafed).

LYCOPHYTES
(FERN ALLIES)

Meet the lycophytes. Formerly referred to as *fern allies*, lycophytes are a group of plants that have a distinct evolutionary history from ferns, but they share many characteristics with them. Additionally, the cultural needs of these two groups of plants have much in common. For these reasons, fern enthusiasts also typically study and grow lycophytes. However, despite all their similarities, they are not closely related to ferns.

Experts from around the world joined forces several years ago and published a modern comprehensive classification of lycophytes and ferns. Increasing molecular data has revolutionized our understanding and has led to this new organization of what were known for so long as "fern allies" and ferns. Though not closely related, the lycophytes and ferns share features that no other plants share, being vascular and producing spores in a unique life cycle. *Equisetum* and *Psilotum*, which were previously considered fern allies (they lack macrophylls), are now considered to be ferns, while their former brethren remain together in the lycophytes.

Ferns form spores in sporangia commonly found on the backs of their fronds.

WHAT IS A SPORE?

The ferns and lycophytes (see page 21) are the only vascular plants that reproduce by spore, not seed. Their spores are single cells. They're microscopic and cannot be seen with the naked eye (for a description and illustration of where spores fit in the fern life cycle, see "How Ferns Propagate" on page 29). Reproducing by spore is an ancestral trait, and the completion of the fern lifecycle is dependent on the presence of water. Unlike other vascular plants, ferns retained this feature from their ancestors, being among the earliest plants to make the transition from water onto land.

The lesser-developed mosses and their relatives also reproduce by spore, but remember, unlike ferns, they are not vascular. Green algae are ancient organisms that also reproduce by spore and are most likely the ancestors of mosses and ferns. Although ferns kept this trait from their past, they were the first plants to develop a vascular system. As discussed in Chapter 1, this very significant evolutionary development is still used by the plants of today's world.

Parts of a Fern Plant

Because they are vascular plants, the spore-producing ferns and lycophytes have the same basic vegetative parts as seed-producing plants (flowering plants, conifers, and their relatives). However, in ferns and lycophytes, the roots, stems, and leaves may take on different proportions, appearances, and names.

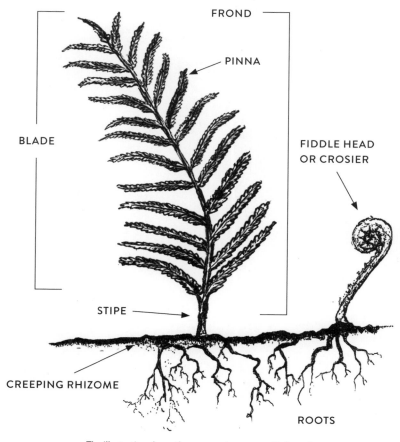

The illustration shows the many unique parts of a fern plant.

ROOTS

Roots, in any plant, can serve several basic functions. Moving through the soil or clinging to the branches of trees or surfaces of rocks, roots anchor ferns in place, keeping them from toppling over, washing away in a rainstorm, or blowing away in the wind. Another main function of roots is to absorb water and nutrients from the soil, delivering them through the fern's vascular system to all parts of the stem and fronds. Not all roots serve all these functions. Epiphytic ferns, those that live perched on the branches of trees, often absorb most of their water and nutrients through their leaves, while the roots serve primarily just to hold them in place. Floating aquatic ferns, such as those in the genus *Azolla*, have given up staying in one place and float freely, using their roots just to help extract nutrients from the water they float on.

LEAVES

The leaves of ferns are called fronds. This word, usually reserved for the leaves of ferns, is sometimes applied to the similar-looking leaves of palms and cycads. Though fern fronds are structurally very similar to the leaves of other plants, there is a specialized vocabulary for describing their parts.

The main, broad part of the leaf is called the blade, and it is attached to the main stem of the fern by a stalk called a stipe. When most of us think of a fern frond, we imagine the classic look, with the blade divided into many tiny segments. Many ferns do indeed have that structure, but it is by no means universal. Fronds can range from simple, completely undivided leaves to multiple compound leaves, with the segments further divided into smaller segments, and everything in between.

In addition to their often finely divided shapes, the most iconic and distinctive aspect of fern fronds is the way almost all of them unfurl. Unlike the leaves of most other plants, new fern fronds emerge tightly coiled and then unroll to expose their intricate beauty. The tightly coiled fronds just beginning to unroll are called fiddleheads or crosiers. Named after the distinctive carved scroll at the top of a violin, the fiddlehead stage of frond development is when ferns are most often eaten as

vegetables, and one of their most beautiful states. For gardeners in cold climates, the sight of fiddleheads pushing up from the ground ranks alongside daffodils and returning birds as a treasured sign of spring.

STEMS

The fronds and roots of ferns grow from the stems, called rhizomes. Fern rhizomes come in two types, creeping and erect. Creeping rhizomes run along or just below the soil surface and are how a fern spreads to cover a large or small area. Some ferns, such as bracken, have very long creeping rhizomes that allow them to quickly cover wide swaths of land. Others, such as the Japanese painted fern, have short creeping rhizomes, and so tend to stay in compact clumps. And there are still others in between that creep slowly and make patches. Some ferns have it multiple ways. Boston ferns, popular as houseplants, and ostrich ferns will make thick clumps with short rhizomes, but then send out stolons (modified stems) in order to expand their territory.

Individual fronds can grow from these creeping rhizomes, or the plants can grow what are called ascending or erect rhizomes. These very short stems produce an abundance of fronds in a clump, producing the classic vaselike grouping of leaves seen in ostrich ferns or the tropical bird's-nest fern.

The appearance of a fern and how it performs in the garden depend on the structure of the rhizomes. Plants with long creeping rhizomes, such as bracken, produce many individual fronds widely spaced over the ground. Japanese painted ferns have short creeping rhizomes, resulting in tight clumps of fronds that spread minimally. Ostrich ferns have erect rhizomes, resulting in the fronds radiating out into a graceful vase shape.

Diversity in Ferns and Their Forms, Climates, and Lifestyles

When you imagine a fern growing in the wild, you probably imagine it growing on the ground, beneath the shade of tall trees. That is where we most often see ferns growing, in temperate and tropical climates and growing in shade is one of their unique adaptations. But shady woodlands aren't their only habitat. Ferns are incredibly varied and have found ways to adapt to conditions nearly everywhere on the planet.

There are many different habitats where ferns thrive, and many ways these plants grow.

- Terrestrial ferns live in the ground.

- Aquatic ferns live in or on the water.

- Epiphytic ferns live on the branches of trees.

- Epipetric and lithophytice ferns both grow on the surfaces of rocks.

Aquatic ferns grow in fresh, or sometimes brackish, water. Some of these ferns grow rooted to the bottom underwater, while others (such as the *Azolla* ferns) live a more freewheeling existence, floating on the water surface. At the other extreme are the xeric ferns, those adapted to live in arid climates with low humidity and rainfall. These dry-climate ferns tend to have thick, leathery fronds, often covered with silvery hairs or a waxy coating to help reflect some of the intense sunlight. They're beautiful, and though sometimes difficult to find for sale, make great additions to a water-wise landscape in areas with limited rainfall.

Growing on the branches of other plants, especially trees, is called epiphytism, and this is how many ferns grow. When people see one plant growing on another, they often think the plant is acting as a parasite, but epiphytes aren't parasites. They don't take any energy from the host plant they're growing on—they're just "borrowing" the trunk as a way to get off the ground and up into a little more light. But life clinging to a branch in the middle of the air is rough. Water can be hard to come by, and in temperate climates, epiphytes are exposed to the extremes of wind and cold, unmitigated by the shelter and warmth of the ground. For these reasons, most epiphytes of all kinds, including ferns, are found in tropical and sub-tropical regions, where winter cold isn't a problem, and regular rain and high humidity make life on a tree branch possible. But even so, many epiphytic ferns share traits with plants adapted to deserts.

How Ferns Propagate

Propagation is how one fern plant can make more ferns. This happens in the wild as ferns naturally spread and reproduce via spores, and there are simple techniques we gardeners can use to speed up that process and make more ferns to fill our homes and gardens.

ASEXUAL AND SEXUAL PROPAGATION

There are two ways ferns propagate: sexually and asexually (also called vegetative propagation). Sexual reproduction is something I'm sure you are familiar with, though ferns do it a little—okay, a lot—differently than animals, namely through their spores. Getting the right conditions for fern spores to germinate and develop into a new fern can be a bit tricky for beginning gardeners, but it is the best way to propagate large numbers of new ferns. Each new plant grown from spores will be genetically a little different, combining traits from both parents,

◄ (opposite page top) Xeric ferns, such as this lace-lip fern (*Cheilanthes*), are adapted to live in dry climates and rocky areas.

◄ (opposite page bottom) Resurrection ferns are epiphytes that appear to be dead during times of drought. However, when rain returns, they spring back to life.

which can be very interesting and fun, particularly with highly variable species such as Japanese painted ferns.

Asexual or vegetative propagation is a lot simpler and can be as easy as physically dividing a plant in half. You'll usually be able to produce only a few new plants at a time this way, and unlike with sexual propagation, each new plant will be genetically identical (a clone) of the original plant. Here's more on both types of fern propagation.

SEXUAL REPRODUCTION AND THE FERN LIFE CYCLE

Sexual reproduction—in plants and animals—occurs when an organism produces cells with half as many chromosomes as the organism itself. Those cells are eggs and sperm. An egg carrying half the chromosomes from one parent fuses with the sperm carrying half the chromosomes from another parent. The fusion of the two sex cells produces a new cell with a full complement of chromosomes, half from each parent, thereby combining into a new generation with a new combination of genes.

Ferns, unlike animals, have a complex life cycle called alternating generations. The fern plants with big fronds that you're familiar with growing in the garden don't produce sex cells. They produce spores, and those spores have half of the chromosomes. But spores don't fuse together—they develop into little plants of their own. Spores grow into a distinct, free-living, and photosynthesizing tiny plant called the gametophyte (the sexual generation). In almost all ferns, this tiny fern will produce both the male and female sex cells (gametes, each still with half of the chromosomes). Once the plant is big enough, it will begin to make egg and sperm cells. The sperm swims through a thin film of water to an egg and if all goes well, they will combine and form a new fern. This baby is the new sporophyte generation and the cycle is complete. The tiny gametophyte plant only lives to produce one fertilized egg and then it will die.

This means that ferns live in two distinct stages. The familiar stage you see growing in your garden is called the *sporophyte*, which means "spore plant." Sporophytes grow over a long period, and when mature, they begin producing structures called sporangia. Most often the sporangia,which look like little brown or black raised bumps, are in clusters called sori and are found on the undersides of the fronds. They release tiny spores, which float like dust in the air, drifting everywhere and hopefully settling in a suitable moist spot.

Given the right conditions, spores will germinate and grow into new gametophytes. As discussed earlier, these tiny little plants produce gametes (eggs and sperm), which fuse and produce new ferns. If the spores from different individual ferns land in the same area, they can cross-fertilize and recombine the genes of the two parent ferns.

▶ (opposite page) This illustration shows the complete fern life cycle, starting with the recognizable sporophyte you see in your garden, through the production and germination of microscopic spores, the development of the gametophyte that produces sperm and eggs, and finally the production of a new, young sporophyte.

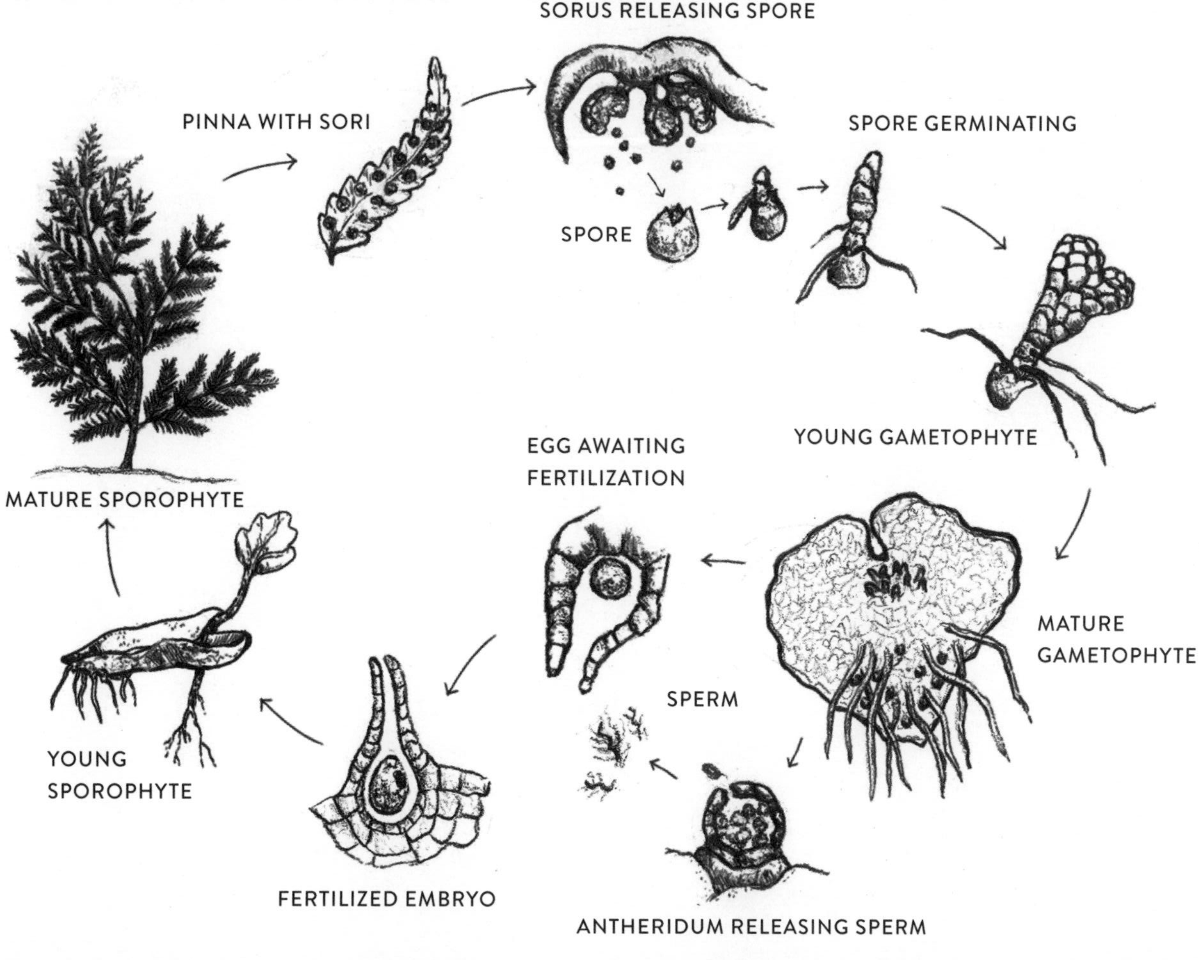

SORUS RELEASING SPORE

SPORE GERMINATING

SPORE

MATURE GAMETOPHYTE

YOUNG GAMETOPHYTE

ANTHERIDIUM RELEASING SPERM

SPERM

EGG AWAITING FERTILIZATION

PINNA WITH SORI

FERTILIZED EMBRYO

MATURE SPOROPHYTE

YOUNG SPOROPHYTE

Ferns of different species can hybridize when their spores grow together. The variety *Athyrium* 'Ghost' is just such a hybrid, produced when a Japanese painted fern native to Asia and the lady fern, native to North America, had their spores exchange gametes. The result is a fern that combines some of the traits of the two parents. Fern hybrids between different species, but usually in the same genus, are known to gardeners and even in the wild, so if you want to play around with sowing different spores together, you might get lucky and create an interesting new plant.

A microscopic view of a tiny fern gametophyte with its new baby sporophyte.

◀ (opposite page) Sporangia are usually clustered into a sorus (plural: sori), which is commonly found on the undersides of fern fronds. Sori look like little raised bumps.

| CHAPTER 3 |

GREENING YOUR ENVIRONMENT

FERNS INDOORS

FERNS ARE SOME of the most beautiful houseplants, providing delicate, lacy qualities, classic forms, and rich textural variety. They are also masters of the color green, showing off its whole range, and displaying variations from gray to blue to chartreuse, and even red and silver. You'll find ferns for the smallest of spaces all the way up to big, bold specimens. There are ferns for every interior style, be it formal décor, casual, or a sleek, modern look. These are not your grandmother's houseplants! Ferns will also reward you as they connect you to nature, bringing the green world indoors. Take a moment and contemplate them. Just exactly what shade of green do you see? What is the texture of the frond like? You'll enjoy the excitement of seeing new growth unfurl

before your eyes, and you can breathe healthier indoor air because of the presence of these beautiful plants.

Growers are expanding their listings and offering a wider assortment of ferns that grow well indoors. When buying your plants, always buy from reputable sources. Plants grown in good nurseries will be healthy, should be ethically grown and sourced, are not collected in the wild, and will generally be free from pests. In any case, give them a good examination before you buy them, and if you can, quarantine them briefly when you get them home to make sure that they have no pests that might spread to other plants. Keep in mind that any indoor setting, including a home, office, or school, is an artificial environment. It

No space? No problem! Pint-size ferns are the perfect fit for tiny living quarters. Left to right: A baby staghorn fern mounted on a tiny tree round, a small, young potted Tsus-sima holly fern, a sporeling of button fern in a thimble, and a lemon button fern in a moss-lined wire cap cover from a prosecco bottle.

is best to assess your indoor conditions and then select an appropriate plant. This is a helpful first step to success. It is usually difficult to change your environment to suit the plant, though, as you will see, there are some adjustments you can make.

Growing culture

When choosing which ferns to grow as houseplants, it can be helpful to have a look at their natural habitat for clues to their specific growing needs. There are five cultural factors that you need to consider when growing ferns, or any plant for that matter:

- Light

- Temperature

- Growing medium or substrate (soil, soilless mix, potting mix)

- Watering

- Humidity

Individually, these factors are like pieces of a puzzle. When you put them all together, you get the complete picture. Because they are all interrelated, changes in one factor may very well affect one or more of the other factors. Another way to explain this is to think of a chain made up of individual links; each of these five factors is a link. Your chain will only be as strong as the weakest link. To keep your ferns thriving, make sure that the environment and your culture match the needs of your plant.

LIGHT

Light is critical for all green plants and is one of the hardest things to get right in any indoor setting. Ferns generally want medium light, or bright, indirect light, but not burning sun. Most ferns do very well in an eastern light exposure. For western exposures, you need to be more careful—afternoon sun can be too strong and hot. For northern and southern exposures, it matters whether you are in the Northern or the Southern Hemisphere.

As a general guide:

- In the Northern Hemisphere, northern exposures are lowest light, east and west are medium, and southern exposures are high.

- In the Southern Hemisphere, southern exposures are the lowest light, east and west are medium, and northern exposures are high.

TEMPERATURE

Most of the ferns grown indoors are tropical in nature and generally grow well with daytime temperatures of 70 to 80°F (21 to 27°C). On a hot summer day, many handle temperatures as high as 90°F (32°C), but that's not desirable. They also prefer at least a 5 to 10°F (2.8 to 5.6°C) difference between the daytime and nighttime temperatures. This temperature gradient gives your plants a nightly rest. Ferns are typically happy with nighttime temperatures of 60 to 65°F (16 to 18°C).

GROWING MEDIUM

The correct potting mix, or growing medium, is very important to the health of your fern plants. The growing medium is the substance in which the roots are growing. Roots take up water and nutrients for the fern, and roots need oxygen to survive. As ferns tend to have shallow, thin root systems, a well-aerated, well-drained potting mix is necessary. At the same time, the mix must hold sufficient moisture and nutrients. This balance is not that difficult to achieve, and it is vital. Most ferns, like most other plants, thrive in a slightly acidic medium with a pH between 6 and 7. Most ready-made potting mixes are adjusted to this proper pH range.

Soilless mixes contain no actual soil, hence the name, and are very popular for use in containers. Standard soilless mixes most typically contain peat moss, vermiculite, and perlite. Some might also contain composted bark or coir. Beginners should start with ready-made, commercial potting mixes, and if needed or desired, customize them accordingly. I usually start with a ready-made mix as my base and then tweak it. Whatever you use, make sure that your growing medium is sterile and "clean." Don't reuse old mixes or dig up soil from outdoors. These may not be in good physical shape, but more important, they could contain pathogens, harmful critters, weed seeds, and other undesirable elements that you don't want to bring indoors.

▶ Pay careful attention to light levels when choosing a home for your fern.

WATERING

The importance of proper watering cannot be stressed enough. Improper watering is a leading cause of death for houseplants. It is very common for people to overwater their houseplants, "killing them with kindness" or "loving them to death." Proper watering isn't very hard to learn, but you must first understand the basic concepts. Watering is intimately connected with the growing medium. If your potting mix holds too much water for the type of fern you are growing, the roots might begin to rot even if you don't water frequently. You can begin to understand now how the proper medium can help you water your ferns properly. Always check your fern's preferences to know how much water it requires. In general, most indoor ferns come from tropical habitats, particularly moist, tropical forests, where there is ample moisture and ample humidity. These ferns generally prefer to be kept evenly moist. Some ferns, however, come from drier habitats and prefer to be on the slightly dry side. Others might want to be kept on the wet side or may actually be aquatic and need to grow in water.

Watering depends not only on the type of fern you're growing and the potting mix the plant is growing in, but also on the size of the container and whether the container is plastic or clay (clay is porous and dries out a lot faster). Other factors include how warm it is, how much light the plant is receiving,

the humidity levels, and air movement. It should be easy to see why there is no single rule about how much to water and how frequently to do it. The best approach is to check each plant daily and water when needed. If you have a plant for a long time, you'll get to know it, and you'll have a better idea of what to expect.

How to Water

When you water, it's best to use water at room temperature. Water that is too cold or too hot can be shocking, even damaging, to your ferns. If possible, collect rainwater and use it for all your houseplants. Fluoride and chlorine are often added to tap water, but the amounts are usually not harmful to ferns. However, it doesn't hurt to fill jugs and let them sit for twenty-four hours, uncovered, to let the chlorine dissipate out (people who have fish tanks are familiar with this process). If your water source is softened, you should avoid using it because the sodium in the water is not good for the plants or the soil. You can recycle water from the basin of your dehumidifier, or if you've boiled some plain vegetables,

▶ Water ferns from the top, allowing excess water to drain out the hole in the bottom of the pot. If the pot has a saucer, be sure to pour away any water that collects in it.

save the water to water your plants—just make sure it has cooled down first.

When you're growing a fern in a container with potting mix, the container should have one or more drainage holes. This allows you to water the plant thoroughly, from top to bottom, allowing the excess water to escape through the drainage hole(s). If your container is sitting in a saucer, make sure to empty the saucer if any water remains a half hour after watering. When watering, don't pour the water over the top of your fern, wetting all the foliage. The idea is to water the soil where the roots are but keep the foliage dry. Apply water at the soil line and distribute it evenly all the way around—water moves down, not sideways. If you have to add water a few times before it comes out the bottom, do so.

Another option is to water from beneath, filling the saucer and letting the potting mix and roots draw up the water like a wick. Make sure that the saucer has enough water to moisten the soil all the way up to the top of the pot. Refill the saucer as necessary until no more water is absorbed, then pour out the excess.

Alternatively (and efficiently), you can plunge the pot into a container of water up to the top rim of the pot and let it soak for a few minutes. Then remove the pot and let it drain fully.

If you have ferns that are not potted, but mounted onto a slab of wood, cork, or the like, it is best to plunge the entire piece in a bucket of water and let it soak for 5 to 10 minutes. Remove the mounted fern, let it drip dry, and put it back on display. You can also give it a shower—literally—for a couple of minutes and let it drip dry.

When to Water

Now that you understand how to water, the question is *when* to water. Periodically, lift your container and feel how heavy it is just after watering. Also lift it a few days later to see what it feels like when it is beginning to dry out. For unglazed clay pots, practice tapping on the side of the pot with your knuckles. If it is very dry, it will make a hollow ringing sound. If it is very wet, it will sound more like a thud. For most ferns that like to be kept evenly moist, wait until the soil is dry on the surface before watering. Lift the pot to gauge how wet or dry it is, and if it is a clay pot, give it a tap. Use all these things to help you decide when it's time to water, and don't forget to look at the plant itself. Don't wait until a fern is so dry that it's wilting. Most ferns are not forgiving, and those wilted and dried fronds will not revive. Forgiving ferns are the exception, not the rule. For those select ferns that prefer to be on the dry side, let them go a little longer. Stick your finger about ¼ to ½ inch (6 to 13 mm) down into the soil—if it's dry, it's time to water. Again, use all the little tricks you have at your disposal to gauge just how dry the soil is. The easiest watering chores to manage are for ferns that like to be wet. If the soil isn't completely moist to wet on the surface, it's time to water. Remember, no matter what the ferns' preference is, when it is time to water, water thoroughly, until the excess water comes out the bottom.

Dormancy

Many types of plants have a dormant phase, and ferns are no exception. A few ferns may go partially or completely dormant during the winter months, though this can sometimes depend on the environment they're growing in. Some species of *Davallia* (rabbit's foot fern), might shed most of their fronds briefly in the winter as they rest, or they might shed old fronds as new ones are unfurling. Any time your plant has shed its leaves in a restful state, or it has been subjected to some stressful condition that has left it with very little foliage growth, be much more sparing with your water. Without leaves, your fern needs much less water. You don't want to overwater and kill your plant while it's in the resting phase. When you see your fern making new fiddleheads and resuming growth, resume watering carefully—a little growth, a little water, more growth, more water.

HUMIDITY

Humidity is an important consideration when growing ferns—in particular relative humidity, which is the relationship

Signs that it's time to water your fern include wilted fronds, a light pot, and soil that's dry to the touch.

between the temperature and humidity. If the relative humidity is 50 percent, it means that the air is holding only half the amount of water that the air can hold at that temperature. The warmer the air, the more moisture it can hold, so as the temperature goes up, it requires more water in the air to maintain the "same" level of humidity. For example, the amount of water vapor in the air at 65°F (18°C) with a relative humidity of 50 percent would be less than the amount of water vapor in the air at 75°F (24°C) with a relative humidity of 50 percent.

As you now know, most of the ferns we grow indoors come from moist tropical forests, where the humidity is typically 70 to 90 percent. Some ferns live in areas with constant 100 percent

Pebble trays offer a great way to raise the humidity level around ferns. Fill a tray with pebbles and add water. The pot sits above the water level, but as the water evaporates from the tray, it increases the humidity. Left to right: *Pteris cretica* 'Mayii', *Asplenium antiquum* 'Crissie', *Hemionitis arifolia*.

humidity. Ferns that grow in these super-humid environments do not adapt well to a home environment. You might be able to grow them in a terrarium, but not out in the open. The best ferns for growing indoors are those adapted to slightly drier conditions in their natural settings, making them more tolerant and better suited to an indoor setting. These include ferns from tropical forests that experience some seasonal dry periods

and don't receive consistent rainfall. They typically grow on rocks or are epiphytic and grow in trees.

Tips for increasing the relative humidity:

→ Get a humidifier. It's a great solution, not only for the plants, but for you as well. Make sure to locate the humidifier where the humidity reaches your ferns.

- Group your ferns together. The more plants you gather together, the greater the humidity in their immediate vicinity.

- Use humidity trays. Put your ferns on trays or saucers filled with pebbles (or covered with a plastic grate). Add water to the tray or saucer so that the bottoms of your pots do not sit in the water, but rather sit above it. This humidifies the air around the plants.

- Combine strategies. Grouping ferns on pebble trays is even better because it puts both strategies to work for you.

- Use the kitchen and bath. If you have enough light, growing ferns in the bathroom or kitchen provides them with some extra humidity from human activities.

- Use a terrarium. Ferns that require very high humidity are better kept in a terrarium. Terrariums are a very fun way to grow ferns with high humidity requirements (see Chapter 5 for a terrarium-planting lesson).

What doesn't raise the humidity? Misting and overwatering. Lightly misting your ferns won't do much to change the humidity because as soon as the water dries, the humidity is gone. Misting ferns often enough to maintain sufficient humidity keeps the fronds wet too much of the time, and that can lead to other negative issues, including rot. It is better to raise the humidity around the plants without wetting the plants themselves. Some people also make the mistake of thinking that constantly wet soil will make up for a lack of humidity. This is absolutely *not* the case. You will just overwater the fern and kill it. For the most part, the ferns profiled later in this chapter tolerate the humidity of a typical indoor home environment, unless otherwise noted.

FERTILIZING YOUR FERNS

Ferns, like all green plants, require mineral nutrients to grow. Growing ferns in containers indoors is completely different than growing them outdoors in their native habitats. With a limited amount of potting mix, the nutrient supply is eventually depleted. Proper fertilization is necessary for any containerized plant to keep the nutrients at levels sufficient for healthy growth. In general, if your fern is making normal, green growth, you probably don't need to fertilize, unless you're trying to make your fern grow bigger or faster. But if growth slows or the plant begins to yellow, it's time to start a fertilizer regimen.

Choosing a Fertilizer

All fertilizers state the percentages of the three primary macronutrients found in them on their label. This is called the N-P-K ratio. For example, a label with 4-3-3 lets you know that 4 percent of that bag or bottle is nitrogen (N),

3 percent is phosphorus (P), and 3 percent is potassium (K).

Organic fertilizers are derived from
organic substances, whereas inorganic,
synthetic fertilizers are chemically
derived and often salt based. Organic fertilizers generally have a low N-P-K ratio;
if you add all three numbers together,
they usually don't go higher than 15.
Organic fertilizers, like those based on
fish and kelp (seaweed), will not burn
your ferns. They are great choices. Plus,
they're better for the environment. Ferns
are sensitive to overfertilizing, and this is
just one reason why I prefer organic fertilizers. Synthetic (inorganic) fertilizers
can also do the job well, but it's important to find one with a lower N-P-K ratio
to keep from "burning" your fern.

Whichever you choose, get a
complete fertilizer (one with all three
primary macronutrients present) that
is balanced. Fertilizers are available
in different forms, including liquid,
water-soluble powder, and dry gran-
ules. With potted indoor ferns, I find
it easiest to use liquid fertilizers as I
water. If you're doing some repotting,
add a granular organic fertilizer to your
potting mix. This provides enough
nutrients for the first two months,
possibly longer. When you purchase a
new fern from a reputable source, the
potting mix likely already contains fertilizer. There is no easy way to know for
sure, but on average, you should expect
it to last a month or two.

How Much and How Often to Fertilize Ferns

Never fertilize a fern that is wilted or
whose potting mix is very dry. First water
the fern in its pot, then wait a day for it
to recover before fertilizing. When using
an organic, liquid fish and kelp fertilizer,
or another water-soluble fertilizer, mix
it at half the recommended strength. For
example, if the label says add 1 teaspoon
per gallon (5 ml per 3.8 L) of water, mix
only ½ teaspoon per gallon (2.5 ml per
3.8 L) of water. If your ferns are in a less-
than-ideal setting and don't ever make
a lot of growth, you can lower the rate
to one-quarter strength. Do this once a
month during the growing season, basically from the beginning of spring until
the beginning of fall. Where I live, in
New York, the first dose of the season is
on March 1 and the last is on October 1.

In areas where the winter months
mean short days and low light intensity,
ferns are in a holding pattern, resting. Do
not fertilize ferns during this time. Fertilizing ferns in the winter only promotes
growth that is not capable of developing
properly under such poor conditions.
Give them their rest and let the growth
cycle start over again in spring.

If you live near the equator and
have year-round growing conditions,
go ahead and fertilize every month, all
year long. All too often, people overfer-
tilize with the intention of helping their
ferns. Resist the urge—too much is not
a good thing. You might hear of growers

Trim old or dead fronds from ferns soon after they brown, using a clean pair of shears.

fertilizing more frequently and with higher concentrations than I recommend here, but realize that they are most often experienced professionals, in the business of producing plants, and they have it down to a science. Literally.

DAILY FERN CARE

Plants growing in our homes are dependent on us for their care and well-being.

Have a look at your ferns regularly, ideally every day, and you will get to know them very well. Do they look happy and healthy? When checking to see if they need water, give them a quick inspection. Do you notice anything different? Bumps, spots, stickiness, and brown edges or tips are often signs of pests or cultural problems. Good plant hygiene is important. Remove dead, diseased, infested, or otherwise unhealthy growth to help keep problems in check. It's normal for an occasional, old frond to turn yellow. If possible, wait to remove yellow leaves until they've browned, as they still hold food and it takes a little time for the food to be transported out of the dying frond and into the rest of the plant. Once fronds are dry and brown it is not only safe, but in most cases desirable to remove them. If they don't fall away cleanly, cut them off, close to the base, using clean, sharp shears.

Ferns also benefit from regular grooming to keep them looking their best. If dust accumulates on their fronds, delicately dust them off or give them a gentle shower. If weeds should ever sprout up in your pots, be sure to remove them. Signs of new spring growth, especially if coupled with stronger light and warmer temperatures, are indications to slowly increase watering, fertilizing, and repotting, if necessary. Low light levels (typical of winter) and/or cooler temperatures are conditions that warrant reduced watering and fertilizing. Observation and showing your ferns a little love keeps them thriving.

POTTING INDOOR FERNS

When you "pot on," or "pot up," it means that you're transplanting your plant into a larger pot. The general rule is to move up one pot size at a time. If your plant is in a 4-inch (10 cm) pot, the next size would be a 5- or 6-inch

(13 to 15 cm) pot. A typical progression would be from a 2-inch (5 cm) pot to a 4-inch (10 cm) pot, a 4-inch (10 cm) to a 6-inch (15 cm) pot, a 6-inch (15 cm) to an 8-inch (20 cm) pot, and so on. Think of it this way: When you're a toddler, you wear tiny sneakers, not adult-size shoes, and your feet grow larger slowly, not overnight. Don't overpot by jumping from a 4-inch (10 cm) pot to a 10-inch (25 cm) pot. It won't save time, and it could even kill your fern because the potting mix will stay too wet, rotting roots and even turning sour. "Repotting" is another term you may hear. This means you are taking the plant out of its container, brushing off a little of the old soil, cleaning your pot, or getting a new one of the same size, and putting the plant back into the container with some fresh soil, but *not* moving it up in pot size.

Signs You Need to Pot Up Your Fern

Ideally, your potting mix should be loose enough on the surface to allow water to percolate down through it quickly. When you water your fern, if the water sits on the surface, taking a long time to percolate down through the potting mix, it is usually an indication that the structure of your mix has deteriorated, and it needs to be replaced. Alternatively, if your fern has filled its pot with roots (this is called rootbound or potbound), it's time to move up to the next pot size.

There are many different types and styles of pots available for growing ferns. Be sure to choose one that suits your décor. Just make sure it has a drainage hole in the bottom.

When to Pot Up Your Fern

The time to repot or pot up is late winter or early spring, just as the growing season begins. Signs of new growth will let you know the fern is ready. Don't repot or pot up a fern when it is entering a resting phase, such as in the fall. Potting up and repotting require the fern to make new growth in order to establish itself in its new home. You don't want to encourage your fern to grow when conditions are not conducive to healthy growth. This will not only produce poor growth but also strain the fern's stored energy supply. Allow your fern to use its food stores to help sustain itself while it rests.

What Kind of Pot to Use

Pots are made of different materials. Choose from plastic, clay, wood, metal, fiberglass, fabric, and even recycled paper. Plastic and clay are the most commonly available. Plastic doesn't breathe

Ferns require sufficient light levels to encourage new growth, but not so much that their foliage is scorched.

and so it will hold water longer and not dry out as quickly. Many ferns that like to be moister, and don't need as much air around their roots, benefit from being in plastic. Clay is porous and allows for good air circulation around the root zone but will dry out more quickly because of this. Choose the type of container you think is best, based on the fern's preferences and your environmental conditions.

Whatever container you choose, make sure it has a drainage hole. Many decorative containers do not have drainage holes. If you want to use one, pot your fern in an appropriate container with a drainage hole, and then set the pot inside the decorative one. Otherwise, find a way to open a drainage hole (there are special drill bits for clay pottery). Without drainage, you risk suffocating the roots, and are likely to kill your fern.

ROUGH MAIDENHAIR FERN

BOTANICAL NAME | *Adiantum hispidulum*

If you live in a temperate area where winter temperatures don't reach below 10 to 20°F (-12 to -7°C), rough maidenhair fern grows outdoors. In some warmer parts of the United States, it has started to spread. This is a great indoor fern, usually not more than 12 inches (30.5 cm) tall when potted in a container, where you can easily control its light and moisture needs. Its botanical name comes from its hairy stems and water-repellent foliage.

CULTURE

Grow rough maidenhair fern in bright but not direct sunlight. It needs some light to prosper but not so much as to scorch the leaves. It declines in full shade. Water regularly to keep the soil evenly moist but not waterlogged. A native of rainforests around the world, it likes high humidity but is somewhat tolerant, so a humidity tray is helpful when it's in a very dry environment. Indoors, it prefers temperatures between 60 and 70° F (16 to 21°C). It's also one of the easiest maindenhairs to grow in the home.

PROPAGATION

Propagate by division of clumps or grow from spores.

NOTES

The new leaves emerge reddish pink, giving this fern another common name: rosy maidenhair. Fronds may color in the fall before they go brown and dormant for winter outdoors. The new growth is brighter pink when the plant gets more light. *Adiantum pubescens,* the bronze Venus maidenhair fern is commonly confused with and misidentified as *A. hispidulum*. It is bigger in all respects with an overall similar look, growing 12 to 18 inches (30.5 to 46 cm) tall. Extremely handsome, the new growth is more bronze than red and it is a little more cold tolerant. This species is widely available now.

SOUTHERN MAIDENHAIR FERN

BOTANICAL NAME | *Adiantum capillus-veneris*

This fern has the classic maindenhair look that everyone loves with fine, lacy, fan-shaped leaflets on glossy black stems. It grows 6 to 12 inches (15 to 30.5 cm) tall and is winter-hardy outdoors in warmer regions to about 10°F (-12°C).

CULTURE

Southern maidenhair fern chooses its outdoor locations in neutral to alkaline soil, often growing on cool, wet limestone outcroppings in shady to partially shaded areas. Because these conditions can be difficult to replicate in a garden, grow it indoors in a container and provide good drainage and even watering. Avoid overwatering to prevent root rot—maidenhairs do not like wet feet. Southern maidenhair fern grows well indoors, tolerating temperatures down to about 50°F (10°C). They love humidity, so place pots on top of pebbles in a tray, adding water to the top of the pebbles.

PROPAGATION

Propagate by division of clumps or grow from spores.

NOTES

Southern maidenhair fern has a history of food and medicinal use in the many temperate and tropical parts of the world where it grows, including parts of North America, South America, Europe, Asia, and Africa. During its growing season, it can tolerate temporary drought, though it may lose most of its fronds. When moisture returns, new growth sprouts from its base.

DELTA MAIDENHAIR FERN

BOTANICAL NAME | *Adiantum raddianum*

This fern, with lovely drooping fronds, can reach 2 feet (61 cm) tall, but in a container it usually doesn't grow more than 12 inches (30.5 cm). It grows well in a terrarium, conservatory, near an indoor water feature, or in any location where high humidity can be maintained to replicate its tropical origins. Formerly called *Adiantum cuneatum*, Delta maidenhair fern is the most common species of maidenhair fern and comes in a variety of cultivars that vary slightly in form, shape, and size, including 'Fragrans', 'Fritz Lüthi', 'Ocean Spray,' and 'Pacific Maid', which is one of the easiest cultivars to grow.

CULTURE

Grow in bright, indirect, or diffused light. Avoid both direct sun, which can fry the leaves, and full shade, which can deplete its vigor. Keep well-drained potting soil consistently moist but not waterlogged. Avoid placing the plant near heat registers or in drafty locations. Add humidity by placing pots on top of pebbles in a tray, adding water to the top of the pebbles. Don't mist maidenhair fronds. Keep the temperature from 55 to 75°F (13 to 24°C).

PROPAGATION

Propagate by division of clumps or grow from spores.

NOTES

Delta maidenhair fern can make a good houseplant and, like many other maidenhairs, often goes through a resting period in the low light of winter. During this time, slightly cooler temperatures, less water, and slightly lower humidity help. Remove any browned foliage immediately to prevent rot. During regular growth, pay attention to browning frond tips, which indicate the fern isn't getting enough humidity.

EAST INDIAN HOLLY FERN

BOTANICAL NAME | *Arachniodes simplicior*

The East Indian holly fern comes from the woodlands of Japan and China. This elegant fern has long, pointed, sturdy fronds with a handsome leathery texture. The dark green, slightly glossy leaves boast brighter, yellowish green stripes down their centers. In a container indoors, it usually grows 6 to 12 inches (15 to 30.5 cm) tall.

CULTURE

To grow the East Indian holly fern as a houseplant, use standard potting mix. When watering, keep it slightly moist. It will tolerate a little dryness better than being overly wet, which may cause rot. This fern prefers medium to bright light. An eastern exposure is best, but a western exposure is a good alternative, as long as it doesn't get too hot in the afternoon. The thick, leathery fronds of this fern help make it more tolerant of lower humidity levels.

PROPAGATION

Propagate from rhizome cuttings, by division of clumps, or grow from spores.

NOTES

Hardy to 0°F (-18°C), the East Indian holly fern is tolerant of cooler homes. When grown outdoors in colder climates, it isn't reliably evergreen and is very late to awaken in spring. In its native habitat, the East Indian holly fern grows from 1 to 2 feet (30.5 to 61 cm) tall on long, creeping rhizomes that don't make tight clumps. This fern is sometimes listed as *Arachniodes aristata* 'Variegata'.

JAPANESE BIRD'S NEST FERN

BOTANICAL NAME | *Asplenium antiquum*

Smaller, but otherwise similar in general appearance to the bird's nest fern (*Asplenium nidus*, see page 57), the Japanese bird's nest fern is attractive and easy to grow as a houseplant as it is a robust grower and tolerates indoor environments well. The main differences between the two are that *A. antiquum* is overall more compact, growing 2 to 3 feet (61 to 91 cm) tall, and has narrower fronds with much shorter stipes. As a houseplant, it probably won't grow more than 1 to 2 feet (30.5 to 61 cm).

CULTURE

Grow Japanese bird's nest fern in well-drained potting soil or on a tree mount. It prefers its rather small root system to be evenly moist; do not overpot or overwater it. Avoid getting water inside the center "nest" to prevent rot. Place it in moderately bright light, such as an east-facing window. Outdoors, it does well with morning light and afternoon shade. If fronds scorch, move it to more shade. Provide extra humidity indoors by placing the plant on a tray with water-covered pebbles. Although it is root-hardy to 40°F (4°C), keep bird's nest fern in indoor temperatures between 60° to 70°F (15.5° to 21°C), no colder than 55°F (13°C). I find this makes an excellent houseplant.

PROPAGATION

Grow from spores. It cannot be divided.

NOTES

There are a number of Japanese bird's nest cultivars, many of them named for people, including 'Leslie' with heavily-forking frond tips, 'Crissie' with irregularly forking frond tips, and 'Osaka' with very wavy frond edges.

MOTHER FERN

BOTANICAL NAME | *Asplenium bulbiferum*

This plant may be the ideal Mother's Day gift. The mother fern, a native of New Zealand, Australia, Malaysia, and India, also known as a hen and chick fern, grows tiny vegetative growths—miniature ferns—called bulbils on the upper sides of its evergreen fronds. As the bulbils develop into little plants, they drop off the mother fern and grow as clones. The plant, hardy to about 20°F (-7°C) and grows up to 2 feet (61 cm) tall but is usually smaller in pots. It has lacy, identical fronds.

CULTURE

Grow mother fern in a room with moderate light in moist, high-quality potting soil. Good humidity is ideal. Remove old fronds for a tidier appearance. As houseplants, mother ferns do well with normal interior temperatures and tolerate lower light levels.

PROPAGATION

Grow from bulbils or spores.

NOTES

Many—if not most—of the ferns sold as mother ferns have been shown through DNA testing to instead be hybrids, *Asplenium × lucrosum*, a cross between *Asplenium bulbiferum* and *Asplenium dimorphum*. This hybrid is sterile, so it can't produce spores, but it willingly creates bulbils. If your "mother fern" displays two different types of fronds (called dimorphic fronds), you have the hybrid, not the true mother fern. The hybrid, probably brought together by an 1800s plant explorer from plants collected in Australia and New Zealand, may have better vigor than *A. bulbiferum* and is just as easily propagated.

BIRD'S NEST FERN (NEST FERN)

BOTANICAL NAME | *Asplenium nidus*

Use your imagination to see the nest: a cluster of unfurled fronds in the center of the vase-shaped plant. In the wild, it's found in trees or on the ground, with fronds up to 5 feet (152 cm) in a clump 8 feet (244 cm) across. As a houseplant, it reaches 2 to 3 feet (61 to 91 cm) tall and wide. Each bright green evergreen frond has a simple spearhead shape with a dark brown rib.

CULTURE

Grow bird's nest fern in well-drained potting soil or on a tree mount. It prefers its small roots to be evenly moist but never waterlogged. Avoid getting water inside the center of the "nest" to prevent rot. Place it in moderately bright light such as an east-facing window. Outdoors, it does well with morning light and afternoon shade. Provide extra humidity indoors by placing the plant on a humidity tray. Although it is root-hardy to 40°F (4°C), keep bird's nest fern in indoor temperatures between 60° to 70°F (16° to 21°C) and no colder than 55°F (13°C).

PROPAGATION

Grow from spores. It cannot be divided.

NOTES

'Crispy Wave' is a variant with very ruffled fronds resembling lasagna. Careful observation reveals that many plants sold in the United States as *Asplenium nidus* are actually *Asplenium australasicum*. However, the differences—longer spore clusters (sori) and differently shaped ribs on *A. australasicum*—won't matter to most people. Both are bird's nest ferns and take similar culture.

JAPANESE HOLLY FERN

BOTANICAL NAME | *Cyrtomium falcatum*

This native of eastern Asia, like other ferns that include the word "holly" as part of their common name, grows glossy green leaflets that show a striking similarity to those of the holly shrub. Popular as an easy-to-grow houseplant, it is also grown in the ground in areas where the temperature doesn't reach below 0°F (-18°C).

CULTURE

Japanese holly fern can tolerate drier conditions than many other ferns and doesn't need as much humidity. Indoors, it prefers to grow in slightly moist, well-drained soil in bright, indirect light. Avoid allowing the soil to dry out completely or letting the pot sit in water. Keep the indoor temperature between 60° and 80°F (16° and 27°C). In the ground, grow it in partial to full shade or in a location that may get morning sun but is protected from burning sunshine later in the day.

PROPAGATION

Propagate by division of clumps or grow from spores.

NOTES

The 1- to 2-foot-long (30.5 to 61 cm) evergreen fronds tend to sprawl instead of standing upright. Its 3- to 4-inch-long (7.6 to 10 cm) leaflets are leathery rather than delicate. Snip off aging fronds when they begin to decline to allow new foliage to emerge. Cultivars include 'Cristatum', with crested frond tips, and 'Rochfordianum', with deeply cut margins.

SQUIRREL'S FOOT FERN

BOTANICAL NAME | *Davallia mariesii* var. *stenolepis*

You may want to reach out and pet the soft, furry gray rhizomes on this sweet fern. At first you won't notice them, due to the attractive lacy, triangular fronds that grow 8 to 12 inches (20 to 30.5 cm) tall. In the wild, these ferns are epiphytic, growing on trees and other plants. As houseplants, squirrel's foot ferns are great for hanging baskets, where the attractive rhizomes may creep over the edge of the pot to easily be seen, touched, and admired.

CULTURE

Grow squirrel's foot fern indoors in bright indirect light. An east-facing window location works well. Grow in well-drained, moist but not waterlogged, potting mix. During winter dormancy, reduce watering to keep soil on the drier side. This fern tolerates lower levels of humidity than some others.

PROPAGATION

Propagate by rhizome cuttings or grow from spores.

NOTES

The fronds of the squirrel's foot fern are deciduous. Expect a period of dormancy during the winter, even indoors, with new growth reappearing in spring. Feel free to snip off old, dying fronds to open space for the emerging foliage. A native of eastern Asia and Japan, squirrel's foot fern is hardy to about 30°F (-1°C).

BASKET FERN

BOTANICAL NAME | *Drynaria rigidula*

Although there is an entire genus of ferns collectively known as "basket ferns," *Drynaria rigidula* is the only one called by the simple common name of basket fern. It's easy to identify from its two types of fronds. The 2- to 4-foot (61 to 122 cm) fertile green foliage fronds that bear the spores are surrounded by 12-inch (30.5 cm), sterile, rust-colored fronds that form the "basket." In the wild, they can even be mistaken for large bird's nests. The durable basket fronds live for several years and serve a valuable purpose, trapping nutrients in their sturdy stems, such as plant material that breaks down into humus to feed the plant.

CULTURE

Basket ferns grow in the wild on trees or rocks, so they make good hanging plants or can be grown in coarse, well-drained potting soil. Avoid waterlogged soils—this fern is fine if the potting medium goes almost dry before the next watering. Place in filtered light. A tropical native, basket fern is root-hardy to about 30°F (-1°C) but thrives in temperatures of 70 to 80°F (21 to 27°C).

PROPAGATION

Propagate from rhizome cuttings or grow spores.

NOTES

A rare but desirable cultivar of *Drynaria rigidula* called 'Whitei', hailing from the Glass House Mountains of Australia, grows with a more serrated leaf than the species. Basket ferns are sometimes called oak leaf ferns because individual leaflets on fertile fronds bear a resemblance to certain types of oaks.

HEART FERN

BOTANICAL NAME | *Hemionitis arifolia*

It's so easy to fall in love with these little cuties. Heart ferns grow less than 1 foot (30.5 cm) tall and wide. Their leathery, deep green, heart-shaped, 4-inch (10 cm) fronds stand on wiry dark stems. At first glance, you wouldn't even know this plant is a fern.

CULTURE

Grow heart fern in bright, indirect light, avoiding direct sunlight. A north-facing window indoors is ideal. In the wild, this fern grows on trees, but it can also grow in a container, in evenly moist, well-drained soil. Avoid letting the soil go completely dry, as this damages the fronds. On the other hand, don't let this fern rot in waterlogged soil. It likes high humidity and is well suited for growing in a terrarium. To raise the humidity under the fern, place it on a humidity tray.

PROPAGATION

Propagate by spores and the babies that may develop at the bases of the leaf blades.

NOTES

A tropical Asian native, heart fern is hardy to 30°F (-1°C) but prefers to grow in warmer temperatures that are typical of most homes, between 60 and 75°F (16 to 24°C). Heart ferns are readily available from mail-order sources.

FISHTAIL FERN

BOTANICAL NAME | *Microsorum punctatum* (syn. *M. polycarpon, Polypodium punctatum*)

The fishtail fern enjoys several other common names, including terrestrial or dwarf elkhorn fern, crested fern, fishtail strap fern, and climbing bird's nest fern. All these names partly describe the unusual form of this evergreen fern's fronds. The 2-foot-long (61 cm), single-blade fronds fork repeatedly, ending in a branched crest that resembles a handsome light green fish tail.

CULTURE

Fast-growing fishtail ferns are epiphytes, meaning they grow on other plants such as trees, but they can also be grown in rich, well-drained soil. Keep the soil moist but not waterlogged. A native of tropical regions, the fishtail fern prefers a warm, humid environment. Provide extra humidity indoors. Keep a sharp eye out for mealybugs and scale insects, which are drawn to this plant and can quickly suck the life out of it.

PROPAGATION

Propagate from rhizome cuttings or grow from spores.

NOTES

Fishtail ferns are hardy to 30°F (-1°C) but prefers to grow in much warmer conditions, from 60 to 80°F (16 to 27°C).

TUBER SWORD FERN

BOTANICAL NAME | *Nephrolepis cordifolia*

There's good news and bad news about the tuber sword fern. The good news is that this is a tough, easy-to-grow fern. The bad news is that it's so tough and easy to grow that it's invasive in many temperate and tropical parts of the world, including southern Florida. Its aggressive growth via thousands of wind-borne spores—as well as underground tubers and stolons—creates dense stands of ferns that crowd out native species. If you want to grow this plant, grow it indoors where its spreading habit is contained.

CULTURE

Tuber sword fern grows in partial to full shade but tolerates sun if given enough water. It easily grows in containers. The evergreen leaves last for several seasons. Clip off fronds as they die to improve the overall appearance. Tubor sword ferns tolerate occasional drought.

PROPAGATION

Propagate by division of clumps, tubers, spores, or new plants produced on stolons.

NOTES

Tubor sword fern, a wood fern that grows fronds 2 to 3 feet (61 to 91 cm) long, has many common names, including fishbone fern, tuberous sword fern, tuber ladder fern, ladder fern, erect sword fern, narrow sword fern, and herringbone fern. Its many synonyms include: *Aspidium tuberosum*, *Nephrolepis tuberosa*, and *Polypodium cordifolium*. Tuber sword fern produces tubers, which is one of the main differences between it and its relative the Boston fern (*Nephrolepis exaltata*).

RITA'S GOLD BOSTON FERN

BOTANICAL NAME | *Nephrolepis exaltata* 'Rita's Gold'

If the ubiquitous Boston fern leaves you longing for something that's similar, but with a little more flash, the creamy yellow to chartreuse leaves of Rita's Gold Boston fern are for you. Similar but slightly different iterations fall under the names *Bostoniensis aurea, Nephrolepis exaltata aurea,* and *Nephrolepis exaltata* 'Aurea' or cultivars such as 'Golden Boston'. All Boston ferns look beautiful in hanging baskets, where their arching foliage creates a highly textured sphere.

CULTURE

Grow Rita's Gold Boston fern in partial to full shade in rich, well-drained soil kept constantly moist but not water-logged. The golden coloration is best in bright, indirect light. Avoid direct sun, which burns the leaves. Water sparingly in the winter during the fern's normal dormant period. It is hardy to 20°F (-4°C) but prefers to grow in warmer temperatures with good humidity. Optimal temperature is 65°F (18°C) at night and below 95°F (35°C) during the day.

PROPAGATION

Propagate by division of clumps, spores, or new plants produced on stolons.

NOTES

At 18 to 24 inches (46 to 61 cm) tall and wide, Rita's Gold Boston fern is slightly more compact than the regular Boston fern. It is named in honor of Rita Randolph, plantswoman and owner of Randolph's Greenhouses in Tennessee. Grow it as a houseplant or as a seasonal accent plant outside after any danger of frost is past. It adds a punch of color to shady areas.

MACHO FERN, BROAD SWORD FERN

BOTANICAL NAME | *Nephrolepis falcata*

Macho fern can easily be seen from a distance, with handsome green fronds 4 to 6 feet (1.2 to 1.8 m) long.

CULTURE
This large, fast-growing fern is a tropical native. It's hardy to about 20°F (-7°C) but prefers to grow in much warmer conditions. Grow indoors in well-drained soil that is moist but never waterlogged. Add humidity indoors by using a humidity tray. The macho fern prefers bright, filtered sunlight for optimal growth. It can tolerate some direct sun with additional moisture but may not have the best color. In lower light levels, it will grow but not flourish. Trim off any dead or dying fronds.

PROPAGATION
Propagate by division of clumps, spores, or new plants produced on stolons.

NOTES
Like many of its *Nephrolepis* relatives, the macho fern can be a bit of a beast, as its name implies. In Hawaii and southern Florida, it has escaped cultivation and become invasive. Grow it outdoors only in regions where colder conditions will prevent it from spreading and crowding out native vegetation. Macho

fern is often misidentified in the trade as *N. biserrata*. *Nephrolepis falcata* 'Furcans', the Fishtail sword fern, which has shorter fronds with forked tips. Zooming in, you can see how Mother Nature took scissors to the sides and ends of each of the leaflets (pinnae) on each frond, dividing the edges and tips into a lively assortment of miniature fishtail shapes.

SICKLE FERN

BOTANICAL NAME | *Pellaea falcata*

The sickle fern is relatively small, at 12 to 18 inches (30.5 to 46 cm), with attractive, glossy dark green leathery fronds. Don't expect all the oblong leaflets to look much like sickles, although it's possible a few will curve around in that distinctive shape. New and emerging leaflets are likely to more resemble a heart shape than a sickle. You may find several different shapes on fronds, depending on the age of the frond.

CULTURE

Grow sickle fern in well-drained soil, kept moist but not waterlogged. It needs bright, indirect light indoors.

PROPAGATION

Propagate by division of clumps or grow from spores.

NOTES

This tropical evergreen fern, native to southern Asia, is hardy to 30°F (-1°C) but prefers to grow in much warmer conditions. Sickle fern is touted as a tough fern for ferneries and terrariums. It makes a great container plant due to its relatively compact size. Remove fronds as they decline to make way for new growth.

BUTTON FERN

BOTANICAL NAME | *Pellaea rotundifolia*

This tidy little fern is as cute as a button and needs almost the same amount of care. In other words, button fern is easy to grow, especially as a houseplant. As you might guess from its botanical name, the leaflets are almost round. Growing just 12 to 18 inches (30.5 to 46 cm) tall with leathery, evergreen foliage, this is a good fern for anyone who tends to forget to water.

CULTURE

Grow button ferns in well-drained soil. They don't need as much moisture as some ferns to perform well. Keep the soil on the dry side, but don't let it go completely dry for too long. Yellow, wilted fronds indicate overwatering. It also has less need for humidity, but during winter, indoor conditions may be too dry. Consider placing it in a bathroom or kitchen, where it may get enough humidity. Grow it in bright to medium indirect light.

PROPAGATION

Propagate by division of clumps or grow from spores.

NOTES

Button fern, a native of New Zealand, Australia, and other nearby islands, is cold-hardy to about 25°F (-4°C) but prefers warmer growing conditions, usually 60 to 75°F (16 to 24°C).

GREEN CLIFF BRAKE

BOTANICAL NAME | *Pellaea viridis* (syn. *Cheilanthes viridis*)

Like its other *Pellaea* fern relatives, the green cliff brake is tough and easy to grow. One of its biggest advantages is that it takes more sun than many other ferns. Cliff brake ferns grow on or among rocks, especially limestone, in various parts of the world. The green fronds with oval leaflets grow 12 to 24 inches (30.5 to 61 cm) long. The plant is hardy to about 25°F (-4°C) but prefers to grow in much warmer conditions.

CULTURE

To grow green cliff brake as a houseplant, plant in well-drained soil. It doesn't require as much moisture as some ferns, so keep the soil lightly watered without going completely dry or completely waterlogged. Yellow, wilted fronds indicate overwatering. Place it in bright, indirect light indoors. Morning light is the perfect indoor situation for green cliff brake fern.

PROPAGATION

Propagate by division of clumps or grow from spores.

NOTES

Green cliff brake fern has become invasive in some warmer parts of the world, so if you live in a tropical area, consider growing it only indoors. It grows well in shaded rock gardens. The botanical label *viridis* refers to its bright green color.

BLUE STAR FERN

BOTANICAL NAME | *Phlebodium aureum* (syn. *Polypodium aureum*)

Some ferns, like *Phlebodium aurem*, just can't settle on one common name. Here are just a few others: cabbage palm fern, golden serpent fern, gold-foot fern, hare's foot fern, bear's foot fern, and golden polypody fern. Attractive bluish grayish green, deeply lobed fronds covered with golden hairlike scales reach 2 to 3 feet (61 to 91 cm). In the tropics and subtropical areas where it grows wild, blue star fern is epiphytic, growing with its rhizomes firmly attached to trees. The fronds erupt in irregular but delightful "higgledy-piggledy" patterns from the crown.

CULTURE

Blue star fern grows in more light and tolerates drier conditions than some ferns, making it a desirable houseplant. Outdoors, it can grow in full sun if it has enough moisture but grows best in partial or dappled shade. Indoors, provide bright indirect light. Grow it in a well-draining potting mix. Many orchid mixes are too porous to provide enough water for this fern, but regular potting soil may be too dense.

PROPAGATION

Propagate from rhizome cuttings, division if you have a large enough clump, or grow from spores.

NOTES

Phlebodium aureum is part of a small, recently discovered genus that split off from the *Polypodium* genus. Most are native to North and South America. It is hardy to 20°F (-7°C) but grows best in much warmer conditions. Cultivars include 'Mandaianum'.

BLUE RABBIT'S FOOT FERN

BOTANICAL NAME | *Phlebodium pseudoaureum* (syn. *P areolatum, Polypodium areolatum*)

Blue rabbit's foot fern creeps around on fuzzy reddish orange to brown rhizomes, flashing silvery, bluish gray, deeply lobed fronds that grow 12 to 20 inches (30.5 to 51 cm) tall. The fronds don't all match, and each seems to have its own distinct personality and form. It is closely related to blue star fern, *Phlebodium aureum*. In fact, blue rabbit's foot fern is often sold as *P. aureum*, although they are two distinct species. It is hardy to 10°F (−12°C) but prefers to grow in warmer temperatures.

CULTURE
Blue rabbit's foot fern grows in more light and tolerates drier conditions than some ferns, making it a desirable houseplant. Provide bright, indirect light, and grow this fern in a well-draining potting mix. It will reward you with lovely bluish gray growth.

PROPAGATION
Propagate from rhizome cuttings, division if you have a large enough clump, or grow from spores.

NOTES
Blue rabbit's foot fern goes by other nicknames, including Virginia blue fern. Synonyms include *Polypodium areolatum*, *Polypodium pseudo-aureum* 'Virginia Blue', and *Polypodium pseudo-aureum*. The botanical confusion comes because it is part of a small, recently discovered genus that split off from the *Polypodium* genus.

STAGHORN FERN

BOTANICAL NAME | *Platycerium bifurcatum*

This fascinating, robust fern grows with two kinds and shapes of fronds, most notably its fertile fronds. These are the irregularly lobed grayish green to bluish green "antlers" up to 3 feet (914 cm) wide that turn cinnamon as they age. Sterile fronds are the rounded, overlapping shieldlike structures at the bases that turn tan or cinnamon. Besides producing spores and offsets (pups), the fertile fronds collect organic materials that feed the fern.

CULTURE

In Southeast Asia where it is native, staghorn fern (also called elkhorn fern) is an evergreen epiphyte that grows on trees. As a result, it needs good air circulation, bright but indirect light, warmth, humidity, and moisture that's absorbed through fronds and rhizomes. When watering, soak the basal fronds as well as the mounting or potting medium. Allow everything to dry between waterings. Both overwatering and letting roots dry out too much can kill staghorn ferns. They look impressive mounted vertically on a wood slab or wire basket but can grow in a well-drained potting medium. Although it is hardy to 20°F (-7°C), wait until temperatures reach at least 50°F (10°C) before moving the plant to a shady spot outdoors for the summer.

PROPAGATION

Propagate by offset division or grow from spores.

NOTES

The large fertile fronds are covered with grayish white furry scales that resemble dust. Don't wipe them off—they are scales that slow moisture loss. Staghorn fern is invasive outdoors in some areas, including Florida and Hawaii.

CATERPILLAR FERN

BOTANICAL NAME | *Polypodium formosanum*

Although the common name of caterpillar fern isn't terribly appealing, it well
describes this fern's odd bluish green-
ish white rhizomes, which are about
the thickness of a large caterpillar, or
grub ("grub fern" is another of its other
common names). Although the most
interesting element of this fern is its rhizomes, the fronds are attractive in a soft
green to bluish green. It grows to about
12 to 24 inches (30.5 to 61 cm).

CULTURE

Grow caterpillar fern as an epiphyte
mounted on wood, as a lithophyte
mounted on rocks, or as a terrestrial
grown in a pot. It thrives in partial to full
shade in moist, well-drained soil. Water
it frequently but allow the medium to
partially dry out before watering again.
Avoid overwatering or waterlogging the
soil. Thanks to its tropical origins in Asia,
it also likes high humidity. The caterpillar fern is hardy to about 30°F (-1°C) but
grows best in warmer conditions.

PROPAGATION

Propagate from rhizome cuttings, division if you have a large enough clump, or
grow from spores.

NOTES

After 1982 when the movie *E.T. the Extra-
Terrestrial* was released, this fern and a
related cultivar with more bifurcated
frond tips, *Polypodium formosanum*
'Cristatum', were marketed as E.T. ferns,
relating the rhizomes to the long, thin
fingers of the famous movie character.

KOREAN ROCK FERN

BOTANICAL NAME *Polystichum tsus-simense*

With its shiny, dark green fronds and serrated leaflets highlighted with delicate, dark veins, Korean rock fern is a charmer. Growing just 12 to 18 inches (30.5 to 46 cm) tall, it is a reliable houseplant. The fronds grow on dark stems, and the new leaves bear a purple cast until they age to green.

CULTURE

Grow Korean rock fern in moderate light in moist, well-drained soil. Although it can take lower light levels, it needs moderate light to perform best. Avoid overwatering to prevent rot, but be sure the container receives ample water, especially during the summer months. Korean rock fern is hardy to about 0°F (-18°C) and likes temperatures to be warm but not hot. Fronds are evergreen, so you may either clip off dead or dying fronds as they occur or snip the oldest ones before new fronds emerge in early spring.

PROPAGATION

Propagate by division of clumps or grow from spores.

NOTES

Korean rock fern is offered as a house gift in some Asian cultures. The fronds are also used in the cut flower trade, where they often outlast the flowers they are paired with.

SILVER LACE FERN

BOTANICAL NAME | *Pteris ensiformis*

Look no further than the common name of silver lace fern to understand something of this fern's appealing looks. Delicate-looking lobed fronds, each touched down the center and along the veins with cream or silver, grow 18 to 24 inches (46 to 61 cm) tall. Some of the oldest and tallest fronds may show a slightly different leaf pattern at the tips. This fern, native to Asia, survives temperatures to about 10°F (-12°C).

CULTURE
Grow silver lace fern in a warm, humid location in bright indirect light to shade. Plant in a sharply drained potting mix. Keep the soil moist but not waterlogged. Reduce the amount of water in fall and winter to let the plant go slightly dormant. Because this fern is evergreen, you'll need to trim off dying or dead fronds to make room for new growth.

PROPAGATION
Propagate by division of clumps or grow from spores.

NOTES
The silver lace fern is also known as sword brake fern. One of the most widely available cultivars of the silver lacefern—and one of the most beautiful—is 'Evergemiensis'. Also look for 'Arguta' and 'Victoriae'.

SPIDER BRAKE FERN

BOTANICAL NAME | *Pteris multifida*

The spider brake fern's name seems obvious when you see the fern. Each leaflet is so slender—less than ½ inch (13 mm)—and pointed that it almost seems as if green, long-legged spiders are spilling over the edges of a pot filled with this fern. A common outdoor sight in temperate or tropical areas, it tends to find its way to disturbed soil and cracks in rocks and rock walls.

CULTURE

Grow spider fern in moderate to low light in moist, well-drained soil. Do not allow the soil to become waterlogged but be sure to irrigate this fern regularly. Reduce the amount of water in fall and winter to let the plant go slightly dormant. This evergreen fern needs an occasional trimming when older fronds turn yellow or brown. It is hardy at least to 10°F (-12°C), possibly colder.

PROPAGATION

Propagate by division of clumps or grow from spores.

NOTES

In the United States, this fern is also known as Huguenot fern because it was collected from a Huguenot cemetery in Charleston, South Carolina in 1868, so it was—falsely, as it turned out—believed to have been introduced by the Huguenots. In warm areas of the Southern United States, it has become invasive. The cultivar 'Corymbifera' has crested leaflet tips.

RIBBON FERN

BOTANICAL NAME | *Pteris nipponica* (syn. *Pteris cretica* var. *albolineata*)

Ribbon fern, also known as Japanese silver lace fern, is a real stunner. Each slender leaflet looks as if an artist took a brush and painted a white or cream stripe down the center it, carefully leaving just enough of a green edge to be interesting. The edges of the leaflets are often lightly ruffled. Fronds reach 1 to 2 feet (30.5 to 61 cm) tall.

CULTURE

Cream-lined Japanese brake fern—another name for ribbon fern—is hardy to about 20°F (-7°C) and grows best in a warm, humid location, if grown indoors. To grow it indoors, choose locations with bright, indirect light or moderate light, and plant it in a sharply drained potting mix. The soil should remain moist but never waterlogged. Reduce the amount of water in fall and winter to let the plant go slightly dormant. Dying fronds should be removed as necessary.

PROPAGATION

Propagate by division of clumps or grow from spores.

NOTES

Pteris ensiformis is known as the silver lace fern or slender brake fern. Unless you require a specific fern, it probably doesn't matter which one you get, since they all shine beautifully.

TONGUE FERN

BOTANICAL NAME | *Pyrrosia lingua*

Leathery, olive green, single-strap fronds with no lobes and velvety, cinnamon-colored undersides resemble 12- to 18-inch (30.5 to 46 cm) pointed tongues. These tropical ferns naturally grow on trees and rocks in the wild but can make striking houseplants. Each frond has gently wavy edges, giving the illusion of movement even when there is none.

CULTURE

In a container, tongue fern requires an extremely porous soil mix. An even better choice is to mount it on a slab of wood (see Chapter 5 for a how-to on fern mounting). You also can use a wire basket with a fiber lining and sharply draining soil mix. Water consistently but allow the soil to dry out lightly between waterings. Avoid waterlogging the soil. High humidity is another key to its success. Indoors, give this plant bright, indirect light. Good air circulation is a plus. It has slight winter hardiness and can take temperatures to at least 10°F (-12°C), probably colder.

PROPAGATION

Propagate by rhizome cuttings, division of clumps, or grow from spores.

NOTES

Tongue ferns, native to Southeast Asia, are evergreen. Clip off fading or dying fronds as they occur.

LEATHERLEAF FERN

BOTANICAL NAME | *Rumohra adiantiformis*

Even if you've never grown leatherleaf ferns, you've undoubtedly seen them packaged with many floral arrangements, often with a single long-stemmed rose and baby's breath. The triangular fronds, which grow up to 3 feet (91 cm) long, are durable, valuable players in the cut flower trade. Leatherleaf is native in a wide variety of areas around the globe where temperatures stay above 30°F (-1°C).

CULTURE

Indoors, grow leatherleaf fern in bright indirect light. This slow-growing fern can reach 3 feet (91 cm) wide and 1 to 3 feet (30.5 to 91 cm) tall, depending on growing conditions. Plants stay on the smaller side if they are grown in a container or hanging basket. Although it is somewhat drought-tolerant, it grows best if you keep the soil moist but not waterlogged.

PROPAGATION

Propagate by division of clumps or grow from spores.

NOTES

This is a relatively easy fern to grow, creating a fluffy yet tidy display. The sizes of the fronds can vary widely. Evergreen leaves look fresh for a long time before they decline. Snip off dead fronds as needed to allow new growth to shine. Keep some on hand for your own cut flower arrangements. Some of its other common names include leather fern, leathery shieldfern, iron fern, 7 weeks fern, and climbing shield fern.

AUSTRALIAN TREE FERN

BOTANICAL NAME | *Sphaeropteris cooperi* (syn. *Cyathea cooperi*)

Looking for a fern from Down Under? You can get down under the Australian tree fern, which can grow as tall as 20 to 30 feet (6 to 9 m) with a trunk 1 foot (30.5 cm) wide. As an indoor plant, it won't get anywhere near that tall, but it will display an umbrella-like set of 8-foot-long (2.4 m) fronds that are reminiscent of palm trees. If you do go underneath, wear protection—the trunk, stems, and undersides of the leaves are covered with bristly brown hairs that can cling to and irritate skin.

CULTURE

Australian tree fern is an understory plant that prefers to grow in partial or dappled shade. Indoors, moderate light is best. It will grow in direct sun if it is well watered but won't be its best. Keep the soil moist but not waterlogged and avoid getting the crown wet to avoid disease. It prefers warmth and high humidity.

PROPAGATION

Grow from spores.

NOTES

Outdoors, Australian tree ferns are hardy to 30°F (-1°C), possibly even 20°F (-7°C). Frost kills its evergreen fronds, but this fast-growing plant can send up new growth. Starting from a low, wide clump, it spreads from 1 foot (30.5 cm) to as wide as 6 feet (1.8 m) in its first year before sprouting upward. Prune off old fronds as needed.

CHAPTER 4

GREENING YOUR ENVIRONMENT

FERNS OUTDOORS

FERNS MAKE ELEGANT, luxurious additions to any garden. Their graceful qualities are calming and they provide peace and serenity in the landscape. As a bonus, ferns are among the easiest perennial plants to care for. The cultural information on the basic needs of ferns presented in this chapter—as well as the information you'll find on how to plant and care for ferns—is universal when it comes to growing ferns outdoors, regardless of whether you garden in a warm or cold climate. However, the ferns profiled at the end of this chapter were chosen for their cold hardiness. They are ferns that can be grown outdoors in temperate zones, where winters mean freezing temperatures. Some of these ferns also grow happily in frost-free regions (see individual fern entries for their specific hardiness).

Although most ferns come from the tropics, the temperate zones are far from lacking in fern diversity. For example, there are more than a hundred species native to the northeastern United States, providing ample choices for growing in a temperate zone. This temperate climate zone forms a band that runs not only across the upper part of the United States and neighboring Canada but continues across the upper parts of Europe and Asia as well. This is why so many of our native plants have "sisters" in Europe and Asia. Having evolved in similar climates and growing conditions, these sister species are often equally at home in our gardens, allowing us all to enjoy

◄ (opposite, top) Many ferns that are available to home gardeners perform well in shady areas of the landscape. They look beautiful when combined with other shade-loving perennials and shrubs.

◄ (opposite, bottom) Dappled shade is best for growing ferns. Try to select an area where dappled shade is already present for your fern garden.

these ferns. However, using native species (plants indigenous to your region), often produces the best results with the least effort. Many gardeners see using natives as a more sustainable approach that's healthier for the ecosystem.

Keep in mind that there are many ferns gardeners have yet to be introduced to. There are certainly far more ferns than can be described in any one book, some of which haven't yet been cultivated, indoors or out. Because of this, we really don't know exactly what all these different ferns can tolerate or how adaptable they may be. If you are willing to experiment, especially with a plant that you don't know a lot about, don't be reluctant to give it a go. It may take several tries before you're successful, but you might find your fern grows happily where you didn't expect it to. Sharing your experiences teaches others and makes us all better gardeners as a result!

What a Fern Needs

Growing ferns in your garden is relatively easy, provided you meet three basic needs: light, soil, and moisture. Generally,

TROPICAL CLIMATE GARDENERS

Because most ferns are native to moist, tropical regions, the more tropical your climate, the broader the palette of species you'll have to choose from. If you garden outdoors in a tropical or subtropical climate, be aware that some of the cold-hardy ferns profiled later in this chapter may not grow without sufficient chilling. See the profiles included in chapter 3 to make choices for your garden. The ferns profiled there will likely thrive outside in a tropical or subtropical region like yours. In these areas, you might also be able to grow epiphytic fern species outside, mounted right in your trees.

ferns prefer some shade, loose, rich soil, and ample moisture. Let's discuss each of these needs in greater detail to make sure you have the best environment possible for your ferns.

LIGHT

It's all about the real estate when it comes to growing ferns outdoors successfully. That means location, location, location! With only a few exceptions, all ferns prefer some shade. Ferns usually exhibit their best growth with bright, indirect light. They do not like hot midday sun. Think "skyshine," not sunshine. Open wooded areas with high canopy shade from deciduous trees, dappled shade where light flickers through the leaves, areas that receive early morning or very late afternoon sun, open, unobstructed northern exposures (in the Northern Hemisphere), or any areas shaded by a fence, house, or even tall city buildings are all ideal settings for ferns when it comes to available light. The deep shade found under most evergreens or dense shade trees, such as maples and beeches, is too dark for many ferns. Avoid sunny, hot, dry spots.

SOIL

The soil is a fern's home. Almost all outdoor ferns prefer rich, organic soils with good drainage. A loose, open soil structure allows for good drainage and keeps the soil well aerated. The organic matter found in soil holds essential water and nutrients and helps to build and maintain good soil structure. Most gardeners aren't lucky enough to start out with such ideal soil. If you can find ferns that tolerate your natural soil conditions, by all means plant them. If not, don't despair.

Fortunately, with a little effort, soil can be improved and amended to suit fern growth. Your soil might be anywhere on the spectrum from dry, light, sandy soil to heavy, wet, clay soil. Whatever

type of soil you have, you can make it more to your fern's liking. Soils that are very sandy drain well and are well aerated. These traits are excellent for ferns because ferns need good drainage and good aeration. Sandy soil is generally loose and open. However, it doesn't hold nutrients or water well, and dries out too quickly. Alternatively, if your soil is heavy clay, it holds moisture and nutrients well but often does not drain sufficiently. Clay soil lacks adequate amounts of air and is not open and loose enough for most ferns. Remember, ferns tend to have small, delicate, wiry, shallow root systems and therefore don't usually like heavy soils. And ferns can't tolerate soil compaction. Because of this, it's best to keep ferns away from heavily trafficked areas and trees and shrubs with big, shallow root systems that compete for water and make it difficult for ferns to grow.

What all this means is that, whether you have sandy soil, clay soil, or something in between, the best solution is to add organic matter. Compost, leaf mold, and composted manure are great organic amendments for improving your soil. Organic matter bulks up sandy soil, providing water and improving nutrient retention, while still retaining its light, open structure. In a clay soil, organic matter builds good soil structure, opening pore spaces and improving drainage and aeration. another option is to choose varieties that are adapted to your specific conditions.

▲ Amending the soil
with organic matter prior
to planting your ferns
is a good way to ensure
they receive good drain-
age and ample nutrition.

▶ Most ferns, including
this Japanese painted
fern, prefer a soil pH
that's slightly acidic. Test
your soil and adjust as
necessary to keep your
ferns healthy and happy.

WATER

Most garden ferns like to be kept evenly moist, and a well-prepared soil maintains proper moisture levels, keeping the ferns healthier and making less work for you. As with any new planting, keeping your ferns properly watered is critical to their establishment. Water regularly for the first year, after which the ferns should be well established. Once established, fern plantings are generally low maintenance and tolerant of short periods of dryness.

In areas with consistent year-round rainfall, you might never need to water. Other areas that receive ample rain during the spring and fall won't usually need water during those seasons. However, if you garden in such a climate, you may need to water during the hotter, drier summer months. Whatever your location, be mindful of droughts or dry spells and heat waves during the growing season and provide additional water as needed. Some ferns tolerate dryness a little better than most, while other ferns prefer wet conditions. It is always best to match the ferns' needs as closely as possible to your site conditions.

When acquiring plants, always use reputable sources. Ferns grown responsibly are healthy and free of diseases and pests. They should be ethically sourced and grown, and not collected from the wild. Never collect plants from public lands or private land without permission from the landowner. Even with permission, act responsibly and check to make sure you are not collecting any species that might be protected, rare, threatened, or endangered.

TEMPERATURE

Once you have identified, or created, a suitable site to grow your outdoor ferns, the remaining consideration is temperature. Be certain to select plants that will survive in your overall climate. Although cold-hardiness is not the only climate-related factor that can affect or limit plant growth, it is a defining one, and it is a longstanding practice to categorize plants by how much cold they can tolerate. Keep in mind, however, that microclimates exist in many places and affect the ability of plants to grow.

For the fern profiles included at the end of this chapter, I've noted the lowest temperature each different species can tolerate. Use this information to determine if the fern is a good fit for your landscape.

◀ In general, outdoor ferns need a minimum of 1 inch (2.5 cm) of water per week throughout the growing season. If no rainfall occurs, plan to irrigate your plants as necessary.

Seasonal Outdoor Fern Care

Ferns are low-maintenance perennials and do quite well with only occasional help from us gardeners. Now that you have ferns growing in your garden, let's look at what care is required through the seasons, particularly in temperate regions.

EARLY SPRING FERN CARE

Early spring, just before new growth begins, is the time to finish any cutting back and cleaning up that wasn't done at the end of the previous season. It is important to do this before the new fiddleheads emerge so as not to damage them. Some people may leave on old, brown fronds as a form of mulch, offering some protection to the crown and roots of the fern through winter. Early spring is the time to cut them away and remove the debris. Compost the old fronds or shred them and return them to the garden as mulch.

Once the ferns and the bed have been cleaned of debris, the best thing you can do for your ferns is to put a 1- to 2-inch (2.5 to 5 cm) topdressing of compost or leaf mold. This should be done annually at the beginning of the season, or you can put about 1 inch (2.5 cm) down now and then in midsummer apply another. Don't work, scratch, or cultivate it into the soil. Remember, ferns have delicate, shallow roots, and we don't want to disturb or destroy them. This annual application of organic matter provides all the nutrition ferns need and supplies the soil with the necessary organic components to keep the soil's food web functioning and self-sustaining. This is all you have to do to maintain good soil qualities.

SEASON-LONG CARE

Throughout the growing season, regular maintenance includes watering as needed, removing weeds, scouting for possible diseases, pests or problems, and grooming your plants as needed. Should any leaves get damaged, break or die, cut them off and clean up the plant to keep it looking its best.

END-OF-SEASON CARE

As fall approaches, especially in temperate climates and anywhere there are deciduous shrubs or trees, you may choose to do some leaf cleanup as the deciduous trees drop their leaves. It's fine to allow a thin layer of leaves to remain on the soil around your ferns as a natural mulch but remove heavy accumulations. Don't, however, leave the crowns of your ferns (the growing

▶ Keep fern beds mulched with shredded leaves or bark chips to stabilize soil moisture levels and limit weeds.

At the end of the growing season, most ferns turn yellow or brown. You can cut these fronds off in the fall or early the following spring, before new fiddleheads emerge.

centers) buried deep under leaves, or they might stay too wet and rot. Be very careful when using rakes around ferns, as ferns are easily loosened or dislodged and damaged.

Many temperate garden ferns die back sometime during the fall. As they turn yellow, or even brown, if they remain upright, leave them intact to add interest and seasonal color to the garden. When the fronds collapse or fall, pick them up or cut them off. Work by hand with pruning shears for the best results. Those who like tidy gardens often clean up their ferns in the fall and compost or shred the debris. However, some growers don't mind the look and recommend that you leave those brown fronds in place. As they lie down around the plant, the old fronds offer a bit of winter insulation. In this case, clean them up in early spring, before new growth begins.

MAIDENHAIR FERN

BOTANICAL NAME | *Adiantum aleuticum* (Western species) and *Adiantum pedatum* (Eastern species)

These two closely related species were formerly considered one species, *A. pedatum*. Although the native range of *A. aleuticum* is west of the Rocky Mountains, and *A. pedatum* is generally in the northeast corner of the United States, the two share most physical traits and cultural needs and are difficult to tell apart. Wiry and strong purple-black stems reaching 1 to 2 feet (30.5 to 61 cm) tall support delicate-looking, bright green fronds that spread out almost like an open human hand, lending this plant another common name, five-finger maidenhair fern.

CULTURE

Maidenhair fern grows in a wide variety of light conditions, from scant to deep shade, and in most soils, from sand and loam to clay. Its unfussy requirements make it a great choice in a shade garden, where it prefers light shade and soil that stays evenly moist but never waterlogged. Avoid placing this fern where hot late afternoon sun could blast and burn its leaves.

PROPAGATION

Propagate by division of clumps or grow from spores.

NOTES

Hardy down to about -35°F (-37°C), maidenhair fern lends an airy, ethereal texture to shade gardens until fall, when it sheds its leaflets to go into winter dormancy. The leaves form about halfway up the stalks, allowing undergrowth to be seen under these frothy skirts. Clumps form slowly, so purchase multiple plants and space them about 2 feet (61 cm) apart if you have a larger area to fill in. They will not grow in the warmest zones. The western species is easier to grow and is the one typically available. The eastern species has fronds that emerge a rosy color before turning green and a more even, rounded outline.

HIMALAYAN MAIDENHAIR FERN

BOTANICAL NAME | *Adiantum venustum*

The pleasing arrangement of teardrop-shaped, soft green leaves on graceful arching black stems vaults the Himalayan maidenhair fern into favorite status for many fern lovers. As you might guess from its name, this fern is native to chilly regions of Asia and flourishes in cool, moist conditions but has much the same look and delicate beauty of the tropical maidenhairs.

CULTURE

This fern is evergreen in the milder parts of its range. Cut back the old fronds to their bases—even if they're still in good shape—before new growth in late winter to early spring to allow the fresh new bronze-pink growth to emerge and shine. Though it will grow in clay or sandy soils, for best results plant Himalayan maidenhair fern in humus-rich soil with excellent drainage. Do not plant the rhizomes too deeply. Keep the soil moist but not waterlogged. It prefers a location with morning sun and afternoon shade, though it will grow in full shade.

PROPAGATION

Propagate by division of clumps or grow from spores.

NOTES

Hardy down to -25 to -30°F (-32 to -34°C), Himalayan maidenhair fern is a 6- to 12-inch (15 to 30.5 cm) charmer that can widen to a patch about 3 feet (91 cm) wide after 5 to 10 years of careful tending and good soil. It struggles in regions with hot, humid summers, even with extra attention and moisture to grow well. The payoff comes from the airy, delightful sprays that add texture to a shade garden. It can also thrive in a container.

DRAGONTAIL FERN

BOTANICAL NAME | *Asplenium ebenoides* (syn. *Asplenosorus* × *ebenoides*)

Roaring to life but raising its spiky leaves a mere 4 to 12 inches (10 to 30.5 cm) tall, the dragontail fern might become a kid's or dinosaur lover's favorite. Native to the Eastern United States, the dragontail fern is a natural, whimsical hybrid cross between two other species of *Asplenium*. In the wild, this fern grows on or near calcareous rocks, making it an excellent choice for rock gardens.

CULTURE
Grow in partial to full shade. Dragontail fern tolerates most soil types, but does best in moist, well-drained soil. Though it is somewhat slug-resistant, these pests may find it worthy of a nibble.

PROPAGATION
Propagate by division of clumps. This hybrid is sterile and cannot grow from spores, except for one population in the southern US. These fertile plants are being cultivated and are helping to make this plant more widely available. If you have the fertile variation, you will be able to grow it from spores.

NOTES
Though the name dragontail is more evocative of its looks, this fern is also known as Scott's spleenwort, named for R. Robinson Scott, who identified it as a new species in 1861. With its short stature and unusual leaf structure, it works well as an edging plant in a rock garden where it can be easily seen and admired. Or, place it in a container where light and water are easy to control. It also makes a good subject for a terrarium. It multiplies and spreads slowly to a clump 8 to 12 inches (20 to 30.5 cm) wide. It tolerates temperatures down to -25 to -30°F (-32 to -34°C). It's evergreen, but cut back old stems before new growth begins in early spring to keep the clump looking tidy.

HART'S-TONGUE FERN

BOTANICAL NAME | *Asplenium scolopendrium* (syn. *Phyllitis scolopendrium*)

This species is native to North America and Europe. The North American plant is *A. scolopendrium* var. *americanum*, and it is very rare and difficult to grow, only growing in soils with lime. It should never be collected! The European plant is *A. scolopendrium* var. *scolopendrium*; it is abundant and easy to grow. All plants in cultivation are the European species. Its common name comes from Europe, where mature red male deer were called harts in medieval times. It's easy to see how it got this name: Long, strap-like fronds unroll, radiating out from a central point and giving the impression of extra-long tongues rising straight up from the earth.

CULTURE

Grow in partial to full shade in slightly moist soil. To keep the soil moisture even and consistent, mulch around the plants with compost, but be sure the soil drains well or the roots will rot.

This fern prefers alkaline soils. If your soil is acidic, amend it to raise the pH or add some calcium. Hart's-tongue fern does not like regions with hot, humid summers.

PROPAGATION

Propagate by division of clumps or grow from spores.

NOTES

Hart's-tongue fern looks almost tropical, making it easy to remember that it's hardy only down to about 0 to -10°F (-18 to -23°C). The 8- to 16-inch-tall (20 to 41 cm) deep green straps rise almost vertically, adding an interesting punctuation to shade garden plantings. The evergreen leaves may be snipped off when they lose vigor with age. Their unfurling fiddleheads were used as the scroll pattern on the necks of violins.

MAIDENHAIR SPLEENWORT

BOTANICAL NAME | *Asplenium trichomanes*

With a common name like spleenwort, this fern could have a real public relations problem. Luckily, it enjoys and shares some of the lovely, airy qualities of maidenhair fern (*Adiantum*) fronds, as well as dark stems. Despite its diminutive stature, it is one tough character. Maidenhair spleenwort appears in temperate climates on all continents but Antartica, clinging to rocky habitats, which is a clue about how it best likes to grow.

CULTURE

Grow maidenhair spleenwort in almost any kind of moist, well-drained soil in partial to full shade. One of the two subspecies, a diploid shows a preference for slightly acid soils; while the other, a tetraploid, loves lime. It tolerates dry shade once its root system is established. The roots will rot if left in waterlogged soil. Its best-case scenario is to find a crevice where moss can keep its roots covered and moist.

PROPAGATION

Propagate by division of clumps or grow from spores.

NOTES

Tuck this little fern into gaps in rock walls or in rock gardens, where it will make a perfect small statement. Soil splashed on the fronds can stunt their growth, so use moss, rocks, or mulch to prevent this. The fronds on this 4- to 12-inch-tall (10 to 30.5 cm) fern are evergreen—just snip off tired stalks when they are past their prime. Hardy down to about -20°F (-29°C), maidenhair spleenwort is slow growing but easy to tend in a garden. Grow as a companion among bonsai plants or in a terrarium.

LADY FERN

BOTANICAL NAME | *Athyrium filix-femina*

Graceful lady ferns bring frothy elegance to a shade garden. Their exuberant growth by underground rhizomes can sometimes move out of bounds in a garden, but they are easy to control and share or discard. *A. filix-femina* var. *angustum*, the northern lady fern, is native to North America and is also known as Lady in Red. *A. filix-femina* var. *filix-femina* is the European lady fern. Victorian England had around 300 named varieties in cultivation, and some are still available. You can find European lady fern cultivars with unusual traits such as cresting (*A. filix-femina* 'Cristatum'), crossing (*A. filix-femina* 'Cruciatum'), and feathery (*A. filix-femina* 'Plumosum' group) foliage.

CULTURE

Lady ferns are no exception to the general rule that ferns prefer moist soil in partial to full shade. But they are amenable to many conditions and may tolerate dry soil but will likely brown out or die back. This 1- to 3-foot-tall (30.5 to 91 cm) fern even grows in sun if the soil is kept uniformly moist but not waterlogged.

PROPAGATION

Propagate by division of clumps or grow from spores. Spore-grown offspring will usually not look like the parent. Spores may self-sow in rich, moist soil.

NOTES

The fronds can be somewhat brittle, so protect lady ferns from foot traffic and areas prone to high winds. By the end of the growing season, just before they lay down their fronds and go dormant for the winter, lady ferns may stop looking their best. Feel free to snip off any unsightly parts as the season progresses. Dormant rhizomes survive winters as cold as -20 to -30°F (-29 to -34°C).

JAPANESE PAINTED FERN

BOTANICAL NAME | *Athyrium niponicum* 'Pictum'

Japanese painted ferns truly light up the shade with silvery flashes from arching fronds that are detailed with burgundy to red stems. They're so popular that they were named the Perennial Plant Association's 2004 Perennial Plant of the Year. Their underground rhizomes system seems to creep out, producing small hedges of 12- to 18-inch-long (30.5 to 46 cm) fronds in a splayed-out, informal fashion that persists through the growing season.

CULTURE

Like its cousin the lady fern, the Japanese painted fern prefers moist, rich, well-drained soil in partial to full shade but can tolerate some sunlight. Morning sun is helpful in boosting the brightness of the leaf color.

PROPAGATION

Propagate division of clumps or grow from spores. It may self-sow in the garden, but spore-grown offspring do not come true and will show a lot of variation, with or without color.

NOTES

Japanese painted ferns naturally grow with variations in color. If you're buying a plant from a nursery, choose one that appeals the most to you. Selections with whiter leaf colors will seem brightest in

the shade. Several named varieties, including 'Burgundy Lace', 'Pewter Lace', and 'Ursula's Red,' feature special coloration on the leaves or their stalks. The most exciting leaf colors are strongest in the spring, with fronds turning greener with hotter temperatures. This is a deciduous fern, so the quality of the fronds will decline as the season nears its end. Snip off old or spent fronds as they occur. The plants survive winter temperatures down to about -20 to -30°F (-29 to -34°C).

HAIRY LIP FERN

BOTANICAL NAME | *Myriopteris lanosa* (syn. *Cheilanthes lanosa*)

Hairy lip fern is something of a unicorn among ferns: It tolerates sun and hot, dry conditions. It's a native of the Eastern and Midwestern United States, and its green, fuzzy fronds and dark brown stems are covered with dainty, woolly, hairlike scales for protection from situations that would fry most other ferns. Despite these great qualities, hairy lip fern performs best when it's not completely blasted with full sun from dawn to dusk. At 6 to 12 inches (15 to 30.5 cm) tall, it's no giant, but it does things most of the others can't.

CULTURE
Grow hairy lip fern in full sun to partial shade. It prefers its shallow roots grounded in excessively well-drained soil or loose, gritty rock with neutral to acidic pH. It also does well in a container planted with well-draining potting soil. Water sparingly but regularly.

PROPAGATION
Grow from spores or purchase plants. Do not remove plants from the wild. The plants may not survive transplantation and they are considered vulnerable, endangered, or extinct in some of the hairy lip fern's native ranges, although they are still ample worldwide.

NOTES
This deciduous fern with brown stems tolerates the cold down to about -10 to -20°F (-23 to -29°C). Grow it in a rock garden, in a trough garden, or in spaces between rock walls. In its native habitat, hairy lip fern is often found in shallow, dry soil in rocky conditions. This is one of the easiest xeric ferns to grow.

FORTUNE'S HOLLY FERN
(JAPANESE HOLLY FERN)

BOTANICAL NAME | *Cyrtomium fortunei*

The leaves on the fronds of Fortune's holly fern resemble those of holly shrubs. The large leaves on upright fronds emerge in spring with a bright, almost lime-green color, then age to a leathery medium green as the season progresses. This 1- to 2-foot-tall (30.5 to 61 cm) holly fern, native to temperate parts of Asia, is evergreen in the warmer areas of its growing range but loses its leaves in colder regions, where it survives down to about -5 to -10°F (-21 to -23°C).

CULTURE
Plant Fortune's holly fern in evenly moist, well-drained soil. If it's left in water-logged soil, the roots can rot, especially in cold winters. Plant in partial to full shade.

It does especially well in a location with morning sun and afternoon shade.

PROPAGATION
Grow from spores.

NOTES
This holly fern was named for Robert Fortune, a Scottish horticulturist who collected plants in China in the 1800s. Fortune's holly fern can easily be grown in containers, as well as in woodland areas. In some areas in Oregon and the Deep South, this fern has naturalized outside of gardens. Though Fortune's holly fern is not yet considered invasive, gardeners in those areas may want to consider this when making a fern choice.

HAY-SCENTED FERN

BOTANICAL NAME | *Dennstaedtia punctilobula*

This fern, when brushed or crushed by hand, emits a scent like freshly mown hay. It also tolerates more sun and drier conditions than most ferns, making it a good choice for areas that may span both shade and sunny spots. If you have a small garden, beware: This groundcover fern may become way too happy and take over your space. It's perfect for an area where you want easy-care coverage, such as the edge of a woodland that's sometimes in sun, sometimes in shade.

CULTURE

Hay-scented fern grows in almost any type of soil in full sun to partial shade. It likes moist, preferably acidic soil rich with humus, but can tolerate dry conditions. If it is grown in dry soil in a warm climate, even in shade, the quality of the fronds will decline by the end of summer. In sunnier, drier, and hotter conditions, the leaves will usually be smaller in size.

PROPAGATION

Propagate by division of clumps or grow from spores.

NOTES

The fine-textured foliage reaches 1 to 2 feet (30.5 to 61 cm) tall, emerging yellowish green in spring, then aging to a light green. This is a tough fern, a native of eastern North America that can survive winters that reach -30 to -40°F (-34 to -40°C). The plant goes dormant in winter, so clip off dead or dying fronds in late fall or early spring before new growth appears.

GOLDEN-SCALED MALE FERN

BOTANICAL NAME | *Dryopteris affinis* (syn. *D. borreri*, *D. pseudomas*)

The golden-scaled male fern shines in the spring when the fiddleheads (crosiers) emerge covered with bronzy yellow scales, as if rising from a vault of underground coins. The leaves on the fronds are yellowish green in spring, then become medium green as the season progresses. This native of Europe and parts of Asia is easy to grow, reaching 3 to 4 feet (91 to 122 cm) tall and wide at maturity.

CULTURE

Golden-scaled male fern is a bit more sun- and drought-tolerant than some ferns, but like most others, it grows best in rich, moist, well-drained soil in partial shade. It is tolerant of most soil pH levels. If you grow this fern in sunny locations with humid summers, provide extra water during dry periods.

PROPAGATION

Propagate by division of clumps or grow from spores.

NOTES

This robust fern is evergreen in warmer regions and semi-evergreen in the coldest regions where it can live. Fronds generally live about a year and a half before they start to decline. The golden scales persist throughout the lifespan of the fronds, lending it a second common name of golden shield fern. Golden-scaled male fern survives winters to about -20 to -30°F (-29 to -34°C) and is a majestic addition to any garden. The complex of golden-scaled male fern that had been classified as *D. affinis* has been re-evaluated and some variations are now their own species. Don't be surprised if you find confusion in the listing of names.

AUTUMN FERN

BOTANICAL NAME | *Dryopteris erythrosora*

The autumn fern is beloved by many fern aficionados—I highly recommend it for any garden. The confounding part of its common name is that its fall coloration is brightest in the spring. Fronds emerge russet or coppery pink, then age to a shiny green for summer. By autumn, another hint of brownish red may return to the leaves. The fall color also is punctuated with red spore-producing sori on the undersides of the fronds. New fronds may shoot up throughout the growing season, lending interesting pink tones to any already established green growth.

CULTURE

Autumn fern prefers an average well-drained soil in partial to most shade, low to medium-high light. Keep the soil moist, especially during hot, dry summers, but not waterlogged. Too much moisture can rot the roots. Place autumn ferns in a wind-protected spot.

PROPAGATION

Propagate by division of clumps, spores, or rhizome cuttings.

NOTES

Autumn fern, a native of Japan and eastern Asia, reaches about 1 ½ to 2½ feet (46 to 76 cm) tall and is cold-hardy down to about -10 to -20°F (-23 to -29°C). It is considered evergreen in most of its range and semi-evergreen in the coldest regions. Snip off any aged fronds to maintain a tidy appearance. The spring color of the cultivar 'Brilliance' is considered redder and longer lasting than the species.

MALE FERN

BOTANICAL NAME | *Dryopteris filix-mas*

The shape and form of a mature male fern has been compared to that of a badminton shuttlecock, with the fronds reaching about 2 to 4 feet (61 to 122 cm) tall and wide. This sturdy fern, native to temperate areas of the Northern Hemisphere, is cold hardy down to about -20 to -30°F (-29 to -34°C). The rhizomes are less aggressive in growth than some other ferns, making it easier to contain in small spaces.

CULTURE

Like many ferns, male ferns prefer rich, well-drained soil in partial to full shade. Don't allow the soil to dry out completely—especially during hot summers—but avoid keeping the soil waterlogged, as too much moisture can rot the roots. If possible, site male ferns where they are protected from strong winds that can damage the fronds.

PROPAGATION

Propagate by division of clumps or grow from spores.

NOTES

The male fern is believed to have gotten its common name because it is so robust and vigorous. It was initially believed to be the male form of the lady fern. However, the two plants are genetically different. Male fern comes in more than fifty attractive alternate forms, including those with crisped, crested, forked, and dwarf variations. It is similar to, and often confused with *D. affinis*, but is deciduous.

MARGINAL WOOD FERN

BOTANICAL NAME | *Dryopteris marginalis*

Native to North America, the marginal wood fern is common in woodlands and rocky ledges and bluffs. The common name describes the location of the spore cases, which are found on the margins of the leaflets. The marginal wood fern also stays in bounds, typically growing as a single 1- to 3-foot-tall (30.5 to 91 cm) specimen. Plant multiples to create a nice grouping.

CULTURE

Marginal wood fern prefers average, well-drained soil and a location in partial to full shade. Though it has some drought and sun tolerance, it prefers moist, rich soil that's not waterlogged. Shelter this fern from high winds, which can damage the fronds.

PROPAGATION

Propagate by division of clumps or grow from spores.

NOTES

The handsome evergreen fronds have a leathery texture and a bluish cast and look good through the winter, even in its northernmost range where temperatures can dip to -30 to -40°F (-34 to -40°C). By spring, however, they may no longer look fresh, so feel free to snip them off to allow the new growth to shine. In the United States, it performs best east of the Rocky Mountains. Besides its use in woodland gardens, planting masses of these ferns can help stabilize dry, shaded slopes.

SCOURINGRUSH (EVERGREEN SCOURING RUSH)

BOTANICAL NAME | *Equisetum hyemale*

Horsetail was once considered a fern ally but has since been classified as a true fern. Horsetail reproduces using spores, but it also spreads via rhizomes so aggressively that gardeners often wish they hadn't planted it. Even a small bit of rhizome left in the ground will sprout a new plant, so it is difficult to eradicate once established. However, used with proper barriers, horsetail is an asset to contemporary, Asian, or midcentury landscape designs. The handsome deep green, jointed, hollow stems reach 2 to 4 feet (61 to 122 cm) tall and offer a unique vertical accent to the garden.

CULTURE

Horsetail rhizomes quickly fill whatever moist space is allowed. Consider planting in an impervious pot with no drainage holes—it can grow in up to 4 inches (10 cm) of water—or in a pot where the soil is constantly moist. Use soil barriers if you plant it in the ground. It grows in full sun to full shade.

PROPAGATION

Propagate from rhizome cuttings or grow from spores.

NOTES

Horsetail is an interesting living fossil that originated approximately 350 million years ago. Because of its high silica content, indigenous people used horsetails as scouring brushes. It is evergreen and survives winter temperatures as low as -30 to -40°F (-34 to -40°C).

OAK FERN

BOTANICAL NAME | *Gymnocarpium dryopteris*

The oak fern is a charming, slow-growing perennial found around the Northern Hemisphere. Its rhizomes creep slowly, so it's easy to control and makes a beautiful ground cover. Rarely reaching more than 1 foot (30.5 cm) tall, it sports delicate-looking, triangular, horizontal fronds that emerge in spring. The foliage starts out a light apple green color that ages to a medium green. Oak ferns produce new fronds throughout the growing season. Oddly, despite the common name, oak ferns are not found growing near oak trees, nor do their fronds resemble oak leaves.

CULTURE

Oak fern grows best in well-drained, moist soil in partial to full shade. It will tolerate sand or clay soils as long as they don't dry out completely. Offer supplemental watering during droughts.

PROPAGATION

Propagate by division of clumps, from rhizome cuttings, or grow from spores.

NOTES

The crushed fronds of oak ferns were used in earlier times to repel mosquitoes and treat bites. This deciduous fern's good looks are likely to fade as the growing season progresses, especially in areas of hot, dry summers. Feel free to snip off any dying fronds for a tidier appearance. A boon to Northern gardeners, oak fern is a truly tough plant that survives winters as cold as -40 to -50°F (-40 to 46°C).

NETTED CHAIN FERN

BOTANICAL NAME | *Lorinseria areolata* (syn. *Woodwardia areolata*)

Netted chain fern, native to eastern North America, is a swamp- and bog-loving fern. Take a good close look at its wide green leaflets to see the netted veining pattern. This fern has separate sterile and fertile fronds. The other part of the common name comes from fertile fronds that carry spores arranged in chainlike rows. This 18- to 24-inch-tall (46 to 61 cm) fern can multiply into large colonies in wet ground, thanks to its rampant rhizomes.

CULTURE

Grow netted chain fern in a bog, pond-side, or in rich, well-drained soils in partial to full shade. It can take more sun if the soil is kept consistently moist. Moisture is key to keeping this fern alive.

PROPAGATION

Propagate by dividing clumps if they're large enough, from rhizome cuttings, or grow from spores.

NOTES

This fern is similar in appearance to the sensitive fern (*Onoclea sensibilis*, page 109). However, sensitive ferns are more common and generally 12 to 24 inches (30.5 to 61 cm) taller, with smooth leaflets and beaded fertile fronds. Netted chain fern is deciduous, shedding its leaves by the end of the season. Clip off old or dead fronds to make way for the following spring's bronze-colored growth. It is a tough perennial, surviving winters that can reach -30 to -40°F (-34 to -40°C).

OSTRICH FERN

BOTANICAL NAME | *Matteuccia struthiopteris* (syn. *M. pensylvanica, Struthiopteris pensylvanica, Pteretis nodulosa*)

Ostrich fern is a happy-go-lucky, super-hardy perennial, ready to romp through as much space as you can give it in the cooler regions of its native North America. It is most exuberant in moist shade, but also growns in wet areas. This tendency to run and form massive colonies makes it difficult to contain in small gardens. It's also a monster: The fronds can reach up to 6 feet (1.8 m) tall when it grows in moist and cool conditions in the wild. Ostrich fern produces tight fiddleheads that are often harvested and cooked—they should not be consumed raw—as a spring delicacy. When left to grow to maturity, the huge, feathery fronds resemble the plumes of its namesake flightless bird.

CULTURE

Grow ostrich ferns in moist, rich, well-drained soil with almost any pH. Don't be surprised if the fronds of the ostrich fern, which look so magnificent in spring, decline during dry spells. They don't grow well in hot areas. The fronds can easily be beaten down by wind and hail.

PROPAGATION

Propagate by division of clumps, by seperating new plants formed on stolons, or grow from spores.

NOTES

This is a deciduous fern, so even if the fronds maintain their appearance over the growing season, expect them to die back in time for winter dormancy. The separate fertile fronds are brown and woody looking; they persist through the winter and provide decorative interest. It survives winters down to -30 to -40°F (-34 to -40°C).

SENSITIVE FERN

BOTANICAL NAME | *Onoclea sensibilis*

No, the sensitive fern doesn't quiver and close when you touch it. The common name comes from this deciduous fern's quick response to frost. It immediately shifts colors from green to brown. Once you learn about them, it's easy to identify sensitive ferns because of the distinctive profiles of the fronds. The nonfertile fronds carry rather large serrated medium green leaves that don't emerge in spring until the danger of frost has passed. The fertile fronds don't bear leaves at all, but resemble stalks with small, dark brown beads. These beadlike structures hold the spores made in the summer and release them the following winter, giving this fern another common name: bead fern.

CULTURE

Sensitive ferns prefer to grow in partial to full shade but tolerate full sun if given enough moisture. Shelter plants from strong winds. In the wild, they grow well in disturbed areas along wetlands. The rhizomes can multiply quickly in ideal conditions, so control them quickly if they're getting out of bounds.

PROPAGATION

Propagate by division of clumps, from rhizome cuttings, or grow from spores.

NOTES

Sensitive ferns, native in many cooler parts of the Northern Hemisphere, appear to have originated millions of years ago, based on fossil imprints. It reaches 2 feet (61 cm) tall and wide and survives winters down to -20 to -40°F (-29 to -40°C).

ROYAL FERN

BOTANICAL NAME | *Osmunda regalis*

The royal fern is a regal addition to any shade garden. It has a distinctive appearance, with fleshy, rounded leaflets that more closely resemble members of the pea family or black locust trees (*Robinia*) instead of ferns. The fertile fronds of the royal fern are located on upright brown fronds that give it another common name: flowering fern.

CULTURE

Royal fern thrives on moisture and grows well in boggy areas or near wooded streams and ponds. With constant moisture and partial shade, it can reach 6 feet (1.8 m) tall or more. Despite its love of water, the royal fern is more tolerant of sun than many other ferns and can be drought tolerant. More sun and less moisture, however, produces smaller plants. In warmer climates, plant royal ferns in partial to full shade.

PROPAGATION

Propagate by division of clumps or grow from spores.

NOTES

Royal fern has two varieties, one native to Europe and Asia, the other native to North America. The European variety, *Osmunda regalis* var. *regalis* is usually larger and more robust, has more leathery leaflets, and typically stays green until

freezing weather, whereas the North American one, *Osmunda regalis* var. *spectabilis*, tends to be smaller and more slender in appearance and turns yellow as cold approaches. Both slow-growing ferns grow in many parts of the world, surviving winters that reach from -30 to -40°F (-34 to -40°C), possibly colder.

CINNAMON FERN

BOTANICAL NAME | *Osmundastrum cinnamomeum* (syn. *Osmunda cinnamomea*)

The cinnamon fern, perhaps unfortunately, does not smell like cinnamon. But the rust-colored, spore-bearing, fertile fronds certainly mimic the color as they stand like stiff and slender soldiers among the 2- to 4-foot (61 to 122 cm), vase-shaped, sterile green fronds. In the fall, the sterile fronds turn from green to yellow before these deciduous ferns go dormant for the winter. By summer, the fertile fronds will have released their spores and died back. The plant can survive winter temperatures down to -30 to -40°F (-34 to -40°C).

CULTURE

Grow cinnamon ferns in moist, well-drained neutral to acid soil in partial to full shade. Dappled or filtered shade is best. In its native habitat, it likes to grow in wetlands, making it a good choice to grow along ponds, streams, and water gardens. If grown in hot, dry shade without supplemental water, this fern's fronds will quickly begin a downward slide toward dormancy, by late summer if not earlier.

PROPAGATION

Propagate by division of clumps or grow from spores.

NOTES

The cinnamon in the common name refers to the dense upright clusters of cinnamon-colored spores. Cinnamon fern is not overly aggressive.

LICORICE FERN (SWEET ROOT FERN)

BOTANICAL NAME | *Polypodium glycyrrhiza*

The licorice fern is a bit of a surprise. Its botanical name describes a couple of this fern's many unusual qualities. *Polypodium* means "many footed," so instead of originating all its fronds from one central spot, licorice fern grows its fronds at random points along its creeping rhizomes. The word *glycyrrhiza* refers to the sweet (*glykys* from Greek) licorice flavor of its rhizomes (*rhiza*, meaning root). Indigenous peoples used these tasty roots for flavoring and medicines. Another interesting trait: Licorice fern is dormant during the summer but begins growing leathery green fronds again from early fall through spring in the temperate and tropical climates where it is native. Finally, it is epiphytic, meaning its roots don't need to be grown in soil but can cling to vertical surfaces, such as moss-covered rocks or trees.

CULTURE

Grow licorice fern in partial to full shade. It will grow in moist soil but can clamber up trees, especially maples, or rock faces on which moss grows naturally. The moisture-retaining moss helps to cool and protect its shallow root system.

PROPAGATION

Propagate from rhizome cuttings or grow from spores.

NOTES

This unusual, 1- to 2-foot–tall (30.5 to 61 cm) fern is native to the Pacific Northwest and prefers areas with cool, moist summers and warm, wet winters. It grows only where winter temperatures dip no lower than -10°F (-23°C).

CHRISTMAS FERN

BOTANICAL NAME | *Polystichum acrostichoides*

They may not get decorated with ornaments and lights, but Christmas fern fronds stay evergreen, even when lying flat under a heap of snow. The 1- to 2-foot (30.5 to 61 cm), leathery green fronds are often used in holiday floral arrangements. This hardy fern grows in many places, surviving winters with temperatures down to -30 to -40°F (-34 to -40°C). It grows mainly east of the Rocky Mountains in the United States. A relative, the Western sword fern *Polystichum munitum* (see page 115), fills the same role west of the Rockies.

CULTURE

Grow Christmas fern in rich, well-drained soil in partial to full shade. Plant the crown of this fern at an angle to prevent water or snowmelt from collecting inside and rotting the plant. Though they thrive with good soil and adequate moisture, keep once established, Christmas ferns can survive in drought conditions in clay soil or rubble and tolerate deeper shade. Snip off old fronds in spring before new ones emerge.

PROPAGATION

Propagate by division of clumps or grow from spores.

NOTES

The size of the clumps increases over time, but although this fern grows rhizomes, the roots don't spread much beyond one to three clumps. When planted in masses on a shady hillside, Christmas ferns are helpful in controlling soil erosion.

MAKINO'S HOLLY FERN

BOTANICAL NAME | *Polystichum makinoi*

Makino's holly fern is something of a darling in the horticulture world, with good reason: It's a real looker. Satiny to glossy olive-green, arching fronds adorn sturdy, stiff stems covered with attractive dark brown scales. The 1- to 2-foot-tall (30.5 to 61 cm) tidy clumps seem more elegant and prepossessing than some other types of ferns. It's a great garden choice used alone as a specimen or massed for effect. It also performs well in a container located in a shady spot. In the garden, its lacy texture works well as a foil against shade plants with broad leaves. Pair its olive color against deep green or variegated gold-green foliage.

CULTURE

Makino's holly fern prefers to grow in rich, moist, well-drained soil, but can tolerate clay or sandy soils. It tolerates hot, dry summer weather but fares better if offered supplemental water during periods of drought. It grows in partial to full shade.

PROPAGATION

Propagate by division of clumps or grow from spores.

NOTES

This Asian native is considered evergreen. The previous year's growth will decline after new fronds appear, so clip back the old fronds in late winter to early spring. Makino's holly fern survives winters that reach as cold as -10 to -20°F (-23 to -29°C).

WESTERN SWORD FERN

BOTANICAL NAME | *Polystichum munitum*

If they were forged into actual swords of human size, the individual serrated leaflets of the western sword fern would indeed be mighty. But even with fronds, this fern is a mighty presence in the shade of natural and cultivated gardens in the Western United States, the Pacific Northwest, and adjacent areas of Canada. It refuses to grow well east of the Rocky Mountains but its relative the Christmas fern, *Polystichum acrostichoides*, takes over from there. (See page 113). Evergreen clumps of fronds that grow from about 4 feet (1.2 m) to nearly 6 feet (1.8 m) long make this a fern to reckon with.

CULTURE

Grow the Western sword fern in a woodland setting in partial to full shade, where it has plenty of room to spread out. In locations with more sun, the plant grows more upright, with shorter fronds. It grows best in rich, well-drained, acidic soil. This fern survives occasional drought but needs supplemental water to look its best. It prefers cooler weather and consistent moisture.

PROPAGATION

Propagate by division of clumps or grow from spores.

NOTES

Western sword fern survives winter temperatures down to about 0 to -10°F (-18 to -23°C). When new growth appears in spring, check the old fronds. Remove any that are declining in appearance, unless you want them to remain to decompose and augment the soil.

ARBORVITAE FERN OR BRAUN'S SPIKEMOSS

BOTANICAL NAME | *Selaginella braunii*

Selaginella braunii masquerades as a fern, but it is really a spikemoss, a member of a group of plants called lycophytes or fern allies. Lycophytes, which were outlined in Chapter 2, are nonflowering plants that reproduce via spores. Arborvitae fern looks like a cross between a fern and a dwarf conifer. Its upright green, lacy fronds resemble the foliage of an arborvitae evergreen. Grow it for its unusual foliage, which adds texture in a shade garden planted with broad-leaved plants such as hostas.

CULTURE

This 6- to 18-inch (15 to 46 cm) charmer grows from very slowly spreading rhizomes, forming a 2-foot-wide (61 cm) clump in about 3 years. It prefers moist, well-drained soil in partial to full shade, although it can tolerate drier soil once it is established. As with other ferns, offer supplemental water during periods of drought.

PROPAGATION

Propagate by division of clumps.

NOTES

Arborvitae fern's foliage is evergreen in warmer climates, semi-evergreen and bronze colored in cooler regions, and may turn brown in the coldest areas. The fronds, late to emerge in spring, are a bright green color, then turn a darker green in fall. This plant is not a fan of cold regions, though it will survive in winters that reach 0 to -10°F (-18 to -23°C).

NEW YORK FERN

BOTANICAL NAME | *Thelypteris noveboracensis* (syn. *Parathelypteris noveboracensis*)

Start spreading the news: The New York fern is an excellent spreading ground-cover if you have lots of space. Its 1- to 2-foot (30.5 to 61 cm) lacy green fronds are readily identifiable by their distinctive shapes. They are tapered at both ends and wider in the middle.

CULTURE

The New York fern is a member of the marsh fern family and loves moist to wet sites. It grows in dappled sunlight to partial shade in acidic soils. It especially likes to grow below breaks in a forest canopy, where it can get a bit of direct sunshine each day, but not all day. It will tolerate some sun if it's kept moist enough. It will deteriorate well before its normal fall dormancy if it gets too much sun or is left in drought conditions too long.

PROPAGATION

Propagate by division of clumps, from rhizome cuttings, or grow from spores.

NOTES

Given its ideal growing situation (acidic soil, partial sun, plenty of moisture), the New York fern aggressively takes over, forming a dense groundcover. If you plant it under trees, beware: Its roots emit a chemical toxic to some trees, especially wild black cherry (*Prunus serotina*). This deciduous fern achieves yellow fall color before it dies back to the ground. Its rhizomes survive winter temperatures in the range of -20 to -30°F (-29 to -34°C).

| CHAPTER 5 |

DO-IT-YOURSELF CRAFTING WITH FERNS

NOW THAT you've learned all about ferns and how to select which ones to grow, it's time to let your creative juices flow. The following pages are filled with fun, fresh, and inspiring ways to display your new fronds. These DIY projects allow you to express your own unique style as you design each individual piece to complement your personal space.

For all the following projects, please source plants responsibly. Never dig plants or harvest fronds from the wild.

Purchase plants from reputable sources, or swap with friends. Use fronds from your own collection of houseplants and garden plants or those of friends, or purchase fronds from florists. Take care collecting, even on your own property. You might just be the lucky one to have a rare or endangered species growing in your backyard! Bottom line: Don't collect anything without permission from proper authorities.

Establishing a Terrarium

Terrariums are essentially miniature greenhouses. A true terrarium is fully enclosed and basically self-sustaining once it establishes, whereas open terrariums require regular checking, yet still provide the benefits of a more nurturing environment than an open, exposed setting. When it's completed, place your terrarium in a bright location, avoiding any direct sun, which will cook your plants. Ideal containers should be made of clear glass to allow enough light for your plants to grow. A true terrarium will have a base of potting soil in which the plants are actually planted and will need some type of lid to create a closed micro-environment. Containers of all types abound—the possibilities are limited only by your creativity. Shop discount stores, craft stores, and garage sales, and look for fish tanks and other items you can repurpose.

Once you've chosen your container, make sure the plants will fit inside. Ideally, choose miniature plants that can survive indefinitely and won't outgrow the space. The trending popularity of fairy gardens has helped make miniature plants more readily available. If you opt to use smaller versions of species that grow larger (young plants, rooted cuttings, small divisions, and sporelings), you will have more trimming and maintenance to do as time goes on, and eventually the ferns will outgrow the space and you will need to replant. Plan out your design before you begin the project.

I simply love the look of a terrarium, and they are so much fun to make.

- A clean glass container with a lid. A wide opening at the top is the easiest to work with.
- A few large stones. I use stones about 1 to 1½ inches (2.5 to 3.8 cm) long.
- A piece of window screening. I prefer fiberglass, as it is nonreactive and very flexible.
- Scissors.
- Coarse-grade charcoal.
- Terrarium potting mix.
- Plants. The number of plants used and their pot sizes will be based on the size of your container.

- A funnel or paper tube. If your opening is too small to scoop soil into place, you will need a funnel for filling the terrarium with soil.
- Terrarium planting tools. Buy some or make your own: tongs, rake or cultivator (fork), scraper (knife), shovel (spoon), tamper (empty spool of thread), duster (paintbrush).
- Watering can. A long, narrow spout is ideal. A turkey baster makes an acceptable substitute.
- If you prefer to wear gloves, I recommend latex or nitrile gloves. Most other types of gloves are too bulky for small potting jobs.

STEPS

1 | Place your stones in the bottom of your container, creating a reservoir for any excess water. Hint: Don't drop the stones, or you may break the glass! Next, cut a piece of screen and place it over the stones. The screen should be the size and shape of the entire bottom, with a little extra to reach up the sides.

2 | Scoop some charcoal into your hand and place a ½-inch (13 mm) layer over the screening. Hint: Charcoal is very dusty; don't stir it up! You can moisten it a little to reduce dust. I recommend wearing gloves and a dust mask if you're very sensitive.

3 | With your design already planned, start adding some soil. I prefer to contour the soil for a very natural look. If you choose to keep your soil level, create interest with varying heights of plants and by adding rocks and wood.

4 | Begin planting. Start with the plant that will be the tallest and at the highest soil line. I prefer an asymmetrical planting, and often place the biggest plant off center. In this case, my fern was just a small division and didn't have a rootball. I simply brought the soil up to the final desired level and tucked in the rhizome and about 1 inch (2.5 cm) of the stem base, as this is how the plant was growing previously.

5 | Continue working outward from the high point and prep the next plant. Spread your pointer and middle fingers apart and place them over the top of the pot and around the base of the plant. Turn the pot over, and with your other hand gently shake or tap the plant out of its pot. Gently

massage and loosen the soil around the top edge, sides, and bottom.

6 | Add more soil as needed and create a planting hole to bring the second plant up to the desired level. Place rootball in planting pocket.

7 | With one hand, hold the fronds out of the way and add more soil with your other hand. Using your miniature shovel, fill in soil around the rootball. Then, use your miniature tamper to firm the soil all around the rootball. Always make sure the original soil line of the rootball is even with the new surrounding soil. Also, smooth out the surrounding soil as you go, maintaining an even grade.

8 | Continue working outward. Prepare the third plant and use the miniature shovel to dig a hole and place the next plant in its pocket. Fill around the rootball with soil as needed, and firm in place. Repeat with the fourth plant.

9 | Add more soil as needed using a tube or funnel. Fill and firm around the rootball. Then finish planting any remaining plants.

10 | Use a miniature rake to smooth and give a final grade to the soil and use a miniature duster or paintbrush to carefully brush off any soil from the fronds. Also use it to clean off soil from the inside of the glass.

11 | Water in each individual plant sparingly. Check carefully over the next few weeks and adjust moisture levels if needed. The stone reservoir at the bottom should never be so full of water that it reaches up to the screen line. Put the lid on your terrarium and enjoy!

Finished planting includes:
Psilotum nudum, Adiantum microphyllum 'Little Lady', *Hemionitis arifolia*, and *Selaginella kraussiana* 'Aurea'.

Creative Terrarium Variations

1. AN OPEN TERRARIUM. Remove your fern from its pot. Place in the bottom of glass container and cover entire rootball with extra soil, letting it spread out and around the bottom. If desired, you can cover the exposed soil with some moistened moss. Alternatively, you can simply place a potted fern in the container. Shown on opposite page is *Nephrolepis exaltata* 'Fluffy Ruffles'.

2. AN AQUARIUM. Use an aquatic fern to create an "aquatic terrarium" in a covered container. It is best to use small, clean gravel, stones, and similar material for these plantings. Source plants and stone at local pet stores or online. Add water as needed. Shown below is *Microsorum pteropus*.

When it comes to terrariums, watering should be done carefully and sparingly. Resist making the soil too wet, because it is very difficult to remove excess water. For the first few weeks, watch carefully as your terrarium establishes. If the soil is too wet, or there is excessive condensation (water collecting inside the glass), you may need to loosen or open the lid to let it dry out a little. Conversely, if the soil is too dry and there is insufficient humidity, you may need to add a little more water. Getting the moisture balance right can be a bit tricky and may take up to a few weeks, but once it stabilizes properly your terrarium will basically sustain itself and will only need to be checked periodically. Remember, however, that open terrariums will have to be checked regularly and will require water more frequently.

3. A CLOCHE TERRARIUM. This type of terrarium consists of a flat base with a glass cover or cloche. Make sure your plant is well watered. Remove the plant from its pot and gently loosen the soil. Place your plant in the center of a shallow saucer (make sure it fits inside the base and cover) and gently press as much moist soil around the rootball as you can, filling the saucer. Cover the entire soil surface and saucer with moist moss (use sheet moss or long-fiber sphagnum moss). Cover with glass cloche. Shown here: *Selaginella erythropus*.

4. A SAUCER TERRARIUM. This is like the cloche terrarium on the left with a flat base and a glass cover that fits over the top. Here, instead of a single plant, I've made a mixed garden. Ideally, the container should be the same depth as the biggest rootball. Use a very deep saucer or repurpose a plastic takeout food container for the job, as I did here. Three different plants make for a nice grouping. Plant them together in the container, filling in around them with moist soil and firming around their rootballs. No need to leave a watering lip. Cover the entire container with moist moss (use sheet moss or long-fiber sphagnum moss). If your container is decorative, there's no need to cover it, but if you prefer, cover with a glass cloche. Shown here: *Nephrolepis exaltata* 'Emina', *Selaginella uncinata*, and *Pellaea rotundifolia*.

Planting a Vertical Garden

Vertical gardening is a new trend. Expanding onto vertical surfaces maximizes
space and adds a whole new dimension
to gardening. As living and working
space increasingly comes at a premium,
growing upward is a natural progression.
Various types of kits are available to make
a green wall: fabric planting pouches,
metal or plastic trays, units with irrigation systems, and setups with decorative
covers or frames. They can be filled with
a growing medium (e.g., soilless mix)
and planted directly, or can simply hold
potted plants. Green walls are wonderful
additions indoors and out. Choose a style
that will work in your situation.

In interior settings, waterproof
planters that have catch basins are most
appropriate. No one wants water running
onto furniture, carpeting, or wooden
floors. Look at your indoor environment—light and temperature—and
choose plants suited to the amount of
light your living wall will receive. Also,
make sure your plants are compatible in
their water needs.

Outdoors, you can use ready-made
products or be creative and make your
own. Choose plants suitable to your
climate and general growing conditions,
selecting those that will grow with the
amount of light they will get. Note that
when making an outdoor living wall, it
is important to understand that plants
growing above ground are more exposed,
and therefore more vulnerable. They
typically dry out faster and are more
susceptible to temperature fluctuations.
Watch your watering, and make sure that
the types you choose can withstand the
additional cold and/or heat they will be
exposed to.

WHAT YOU'LL NEED

- Vertical container. I chose this kit by GroVert. It consists of a plastic planter with a decorative wooden frame. In the back, it has a catch basin at the bottom to prevent dripping. You can also get a basin that fits at the top (also on the back) that you fill with water for ease of watering. It's ready and easy to use. Some types of vertical containers could also hold potted plants, if you prefer that method.
- Standard fern potting mix, enough to fill the planting pockets at most.
- Ten 4-inch (10 cm) potted ferns. The number of plants used and their pot sizes will be based on the planter you use. The soil in the pots should be moist. If they are dry, give them a drink, preferably the day before.

- Decorative moss. I prefer preserved Spanish moss for this.

STEPS

1 | This kit from GroVert comes with all the hardware to hang it on the wall. Decide where you want to hang it and attach the necessary hardware to the wall according to the included instructions. After your planter is completed, you'll simply line it up, with the hardware already affixed on the back, and lock it into place.

2 | For this kit, these special "moisture mats" sit in the bottom of each pocket. Place one per pocket. They absorb water and slowly return it to the soil.

3 | It's best to plan out your design first. You can experiment by arranging the pots to come up with combinations you like.

When you're ready, start planting from the bottom. Remove the ferns from their pots by spreading your pointer and middle fingers apart and placing them over the top of the pot and around the base of the plant. Turn the pot over, and with your other hand gently shake or tap the plant out of its pot. Gently massage and loosen the soil around the top edge, sides, and bottom.

4 | Holding the rootball, set the plant in place. The soil line should be just below the edge of the plastic frame. Check your depth and add soil if necessary.

DO-IT-YOURSELF CRAFTING WITH FERNS | 131

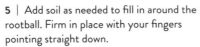

5 | Add soil as needed to fill in around the rootball. Firm in place with your fingers pointing straight down.

6 | Prepare the next plant, place it in the next compartment, and fill and firm with soil. Continue planting, working your way up.

7 | Finish planting all the planting pockets.

8 | For the finishing touch, tuck in moss, covering any bare soil and open areas. When you're finished, water in each plant. Let the planting lay flat for a couple of weeks, allowing the ferns to get established before hanging on the wall.

The finished project includes: *Pellaea rotundifolia, Nephrolepis exaltata* 'Tiger', *Microsorum musifolium, Pteris cretica* 'Mayii', *Arachniodes simplicior*, and *Asplenium nidus.*

7

8

Building a Dish Garden

A dish garden is a grouping of plants that are planted together to create a living arrangement, much as you would design or create harmonious plant combinations outdoors in the garden, only on a much smaller scale. The two most important things to consider in creating a successful dish garden are the plants' cultural requirements and sizes. Because the plants are planted directly into the same container, they experience the same environment. Their roots share the soil, while their above-ground parts receive the same amount of light, temperature, and humidity. For this reason, all the plants must be culturally compatible, enjoying the same growing conditions. It's best to choose plants that won't grow too large for their containers. Otherwise you'll find yourself constantly removing and replacing them, and the planting will always be in a state of flux.

From a design perspective, these miniature landscapes should include at least three different types of plants when you're filling smaller containers, but more varieties can be used with larger containers. Generally, the containers for dish gardens are a good bit wider than they are deep (e.g., bulb pans). This ensures that you'll have room for all your plants without having an excess of soil beneath.

Once you have finished planting, feel free to accessorize with natural items or miniatures. Dish gardens can be relatively easy to plant up, which makes them child-friendly. Gather up the family for this fun project.

WHAT YOU'LL NEED

- Planter and saucer. I chose a blue glazed clay container with an attached saucer 8 inches wide × 4 inches (20 × 10 cm) high. Make certain the container has a drainage hole. A plain terracotta bulb pan with the same dimensions also makes a fine container and might be easier to find.
- A piece of window screening. I prefer fiberglass because it is nonreactive and very flexible.
- Scissors.
- Standard fern potting mix, enough to fill the container.
- Three 4-inch (10 cm) potted ferns. The number of plants included, and their pot sizes, will be based on the size of your container. The soil in the

pots should be moist. If they are dry, give them a drink, preferably the day before.

STEPS

1 | Measure how big a piece of screen you'll need to cover the drainage hole in the planter, leaving some extra to overlap, and cut it. Place the screen over the hole.

2 | Hold the screen in place so it doesn't move and begin filling the container with potting mix. Put in only as much as is needed to reach the bottoms of the rootballs being planted. The end goal is that, when you are finished filling with soil, the soil level at the top will be even with the soil level of the plants being planted. Keep in mind that the final soil line should be approximately ½ inch (13 mm) below the rim, leaving you a watering lip.

3 | Spread your pointer and middle fingers apart and place them over the top of the pot and around the base of the plant. Turn the pot over, and with your other hand gently shake or tap the plant out of its pot. Hint: If you have rootballs of different sizes, start with the biggest one first. If the rootballs are all the same size, I like to start with the biggest plant first.

4 | Gently massage and loosen the soil around the top edge, sides, and bottom of the rootball. Holding the rootball, set the plant in place. Check your depth and adjust if necessary. Carefully tap out the next plant and loosen the rootball. Set the second plant in place in the container.

5 | Begin to fill in between and around the ferns with some soil. Firm lightly, with your fingers pointing straight down.

6 | Unpot and prepare the last fern and set it in place. Use your other hand to gently hold back the foliage of the other ferns. Add soil, filling in around the edge and between all the ferns.

7 | After all the ferns are planted, I like to give the container a little shake. This will settle, smooth, and even out the soil on the surface.

The finished arrangement includes *Asplenium antiquum*, *Pteris nipponica*, and *Nephrolepis cordifolia* 'Lemon Buttons'.

Growing a Tabletop Garden

Tabletop gardens offer a creative variation on containerized houseplants. Unlike an arrangement of one or more potted plants on a table or shelf, a tabletop garden unites many plants together to create a complete small-scale garden. There is no limit to what might be adapted for use as a container for a tabletop garden. Look at organizing containers, boxes, or other assorted items with a fresh eye, and use your imagination.

As with vertical gardens, your tabletop garden container can be filled with a potting mix and planted directly, or it can hold individually potted plants. Tabletop gardens use nontraditional containers—repurposed or custom-built—to create an unconventional, unique look. Tabletop gardens can vary greatly in scale, with larger ones being more "garden-esque."

Tabletop gardens are highly individual and customizable. Unconventional containers require careful preparation, but the results can be well worth the effort. Use or start with a waterproof container so as not to damage furnishings. Carefully adapt a non-waterproof type by lining planting holes or pockets with heavy-duty plastic and sealing all seams or |openings with silicone caulking. Be very careful not to overwater the tabletop garden, since there will not be drainage.

WHAT YOU'LL NEED

- A horizontal container. This one has compartments that can easily hold individual pots. If you prefer, fill them with potting mix and plant directly into them. A container that isn't compartmentalized would best be directly planted.
- Self-adhesive small bumper pads.
- Twelve 4-inch (10 cm) potted ferns. The number of plants used and their pot sizes is based on the planter you use.
- Decorative moss. I prefer preserved Spanish moss for this. Decorative stones, colorful chips, and the like can also be added to your planting design if desired.

STEPS

1 | Turn the planter over and attach the bumper pads. Use at least one near every corner. Add more for bigger containers. The bumpers protect your furnishings by preventing scratches and allowing for air circulation underneath the planter.

2 | Lay out your design before you start. Preview different design options by moving the pots around. I chose ferns with a blue, silvery, and dark green color palette to complement the zinc planter. When you're ready, start by placing the first pot in one corner.

3 | Continue placing pots, one per compartment, until you've filled them all.

4 | Tuck in moss all around, covering any exposed soil, bare spots, and pot edges. For more of a miniature landscape look, you can choose to leave some compartments unplanted, or planted with smaller pots and plants. Fill them with stone or colored chips, creating a "path" or "river" through your garden. Add miniature figurines and props to complete the look.

The finished project includes *Phlebodium* 'Blue Star', *Davallia mariesii* var. *stenolepis*, *Pellaea rotundifolia*, *Pteris ensiformis* 'Evergemiensis', and *Platycerium veitchii* 'Lemoine'.

Crafting Kokedama

Kokedama is a centuries-old Japanese living art form related to bonsai. Translated into English, kokedama means "moss ball." Basically, it is a ball of soil packed around the roots of a plant and then wrapped in moss. Traditionally, kokedama are intended to sit in shallow dishes or be mounted on pieces of driftwood or bark. These days, they are also suspended on strings. A collection of several hanging kokedama make up a Japanese string garden.

Kokedama capture the essence of a pristine environment. Their classic, simple elegance makes for beautiful displays, whether they're resting on tables or shelves, or floating in air. They are also perfect for small spaces.

Ferns are a natural fit, because their variety of textures and forms complement the signature style of kokedama. Additionally, most ferns are not sun dwellers, and because moss balls tend to dry out in direct sun, the ferns will thrive in the more shaded locations for which kokedama are best suited.

Kokedama are absolutely captivating and transformative in any setting and may evoke the reverence for nature that is embraced in Japanese culture.

WHAT YOU'LL NEED

- Bonsai soil. There are many recipes out there. I used a blend with akadama, lava rock, turface (calcined clay), crushed granite, pumice, charcoal, and vermiculite. All these particles are of small size and suitable for bonsai.
- Peat moss, or potting mix consisting mostly of peat moss and a very small amount of fine-grade perlite.
- Mixing bowl.
- Water.
- One 4-inch (10 cm) potted fern. You can also use smaller or larger ferns, but a 4-inch (10 cm) size makes a perfect finished piece!
- Long-fiber sphagnum moss and a bowl of water for soaking.
- Sheet moss and a bowl of water for soaking.
- Cotton string or jute twine. I prefer thin cotton string, but jute works well, too.

- Several feet (a couple meters) of paper-wrapped wire, florist's wire, plastic-coated wire, monofilament fishing line, or nylon string. Wire cutters. The material must be waterproof so it won't rot. Each material lends its own look. Most of them make for a more natural look, but nylon can also be used to add splashes of color!

STEPS

1 | Prepare your kokedama soil. Mix together 1 part bonsai soil and 2 to 2⅓ parts potting mix in a bowl. You'll need about 2 cups (475 ml) for a 4-inch (10 cm) potted fern. Add water, a little at a time, and mix.

2 | When your mix is moist enough, you should be able to form it into a ball.

3 | If you hold the ball with both hands, you should be able to "snap" it in half.

4 | Spread your pointer and middle fingers apart and place them over the top of the pot and around the base of the plant. Turn the pot over, and with your other hand gently shake or tap the plant out of its pot. Gently loosen the rootball and remove some soil, exposing some of the roots without damaging them.

5 | Completely wring out some sphagnum moss as you would a sponge. Wrap the entire rootball with sphagnum moss. Clasp the rootball with both hands and gently squeeze and compress the covered rootball.

6 | Take a long piece of string or twine and tie it tightly around the ball, leaving a short tail on one side and a very long tail on the other side.

7 | Continue wrapping the entire ball, crisscrossing tightly to secure the sphagnum in place, and tie it off with the short tail.

8 | Traditional Japanese technique calls for snapping the soil ball in half, placing the mossed fern inside, and then closing the halves back up. I find this works well with very small rootballs only. For larger rootballs like this one, I find it much easier to build up slowly, packing the soil a little at a time as you work all around.

9 | Once a soil ball has been formed around the roots of the fern, it's time to prepare the materials for covering and hanging your kokedama.

10 | Kokedama can be suspended from one, two, three, or four strings. For the one-string hanging method demonstrated here, first determine how far down you want the kokedama ball to hang. Add an additional 5 to 6 feet (152 to 183 cm) to the length that you want it to hang and cut the piece of paper-coated wire. You can also use a spool of florist's wire, coated wire, monofilament, or nylon string.

11 | Pour the excess water out of the bowl with your sheet moss. Lift the sheet moss pieces out very carefully so as not to break them apart. Squeeze out all the water, again taking care not to twist and tear them. Very carefully "unfold" the layers of sheet moss.

12 | Gently lay sheet moss, green side down, on your work surface. Have several pieces laid out and ready for use. Place the soil ball toward one short side of the moss piece, leaving enough of the sheet moss on the top side to reach over to the center of your ball. Begin wrapping with the moss.

13 | Add more sheet moss as needed, overlapping for complete coverage. Finish by taking a piece to fully cover the bottom. The mossed ball may look lumpy now, but it will flatten out nicely as you tie around it tightly.

14 | Place your wire in the center, on the top, just outside the fern clump. Leave one side the length that you need for the hanger, plus 6 inches (15 cm). The other, longer side will be for wrapping and tying. Holding the wire in place with one finger, take the long end with your other hand and wrap down the side of the moss ball, across the center of the bottom, and back up the opposite side, meeting back at the top. Pulling the wire very tight, twist the two sides together tightly for a few turns to secure it. Coil up the shorter end and tuck it in to keep it out of your way. If you choose to use string instead of wire, tie a couple of knots instead of twisting the wires together.

15 | Now, take the long end and go down one of the other sides, across the bottom center, and back up the opposite side, pulling tightly and holding the tension as you go. Continue wrapping, tying, and crisscrossing until you have secured all around the moss ball. Bring your longer wire back up to the top, and tightly twist it with the shorter end a few times.

16 | Trim the shorter end to 3 inches (8 cm), then tuck it under and wrap it snugly around a section of wire several times to finish off.

The finished project includes: *Pteris nipponica*. This one is ready to hang by a single strand.

Variations for Hanging Kokedama

For a 3-strand hanger:

1 | Decide how long you want your hanger to be, and cut three pieces of suitable string that length, plus 4 to 6 inches (10 to 15 cm). Line up the ends and tie a knot at one end.

2 | Place the knot of the hanger on your work surface and spread the three strands apart. Place the center of the moss ball on top of the knot.

3 | Keeping the knot in the center, pull the strands up one at a time, keeping them equally spaced. You can use a florist's greening pin, or even an unfolded paperclip, to pin the knot in the bottom center if it helps. Pull the strings all the way up straight, holding them tightly together, and tie off in a tight knot at the desired length. Trim off any excess over ½ inch (13 mm).

The finished project includes:
Nephrolepis cordifolia 'Jester's Crown'.

Top, left to right:
Nephrolepis cordifolia
'Jester's Crown',
Pteris nipponica

Bottom, left to right:
Asplenium antiquum
'Osaka', *Psilotum*
nudum, and *Arachniodes*
simplicior

To hang your kokedama with four strings, simply follow the same steps as for three strings, except start with four strands. If you don't want a knot at the bottom, another option is to take two long strands, more than double the desired hanging length, line up their ends, and fold in half. Use a small twist tie, florist's greening pin, or unfolded paper clip and secure the folded point in the center, on the bottom of the moss ball. Bring your strings up, equally spaced, pull them straight and taut, hold the loose ends together, and tie a knot.

Two-string hanging is another option, but with the two-string method it's harder to get your kokedama to hang straight. Cut two strings a little longer than the desired hanging length. Tie the first string onto one side of the moss ball, attaching it to several pieces that you tied around the moss. Then tie the second string to the opposite side. Pull them both up straight and taut, so that your kokedama is level, and tie them off in a knot.

For a monofilament hanger:

Monofilament is not very visible and can make your kokedama appear as if they are floating in air, especially if you use a single string. Take note that monofilament also requires particular knotting practices (see below). Nylon string can provide color. Choose a color to match your décor or make every strand different for a rainbow effect.

Using the three-string method is the easiest for making a monofilament hanger. To tie the strings together at the bottom, use an overhand knot twice. For a loop at the top of your hanging strands, tie all three together in an overhand knot twice, but cinch them tight while keeping a little loop open. For working with a single string, practice tying an improved clinch knot.

This planting includes *Asplenium antiquum* 'Osaka' and *Arachniodes simplicior*.

MOSS BASKETS, MOUNTS, AND MOSS POLES

The sphagnum moss used in the following three projects grows in bogs. Bogs are wet, acidic, and anaerobic environments. Under these conditions, things decay at an extremely slow rate, and the decaying matter continues to build up in layers over very long periods of time. The deep layers are where peat moss comes from. On occasion, bog bodies have been discovered in peat bogs. One of the oldest is the Haraldskaer Woman from Denmark; she lived around 490 BCE.

Sphagnum moss, living or dead, is very absorptive and extremely acidic, which inhibits the growth of bacteria and fungi. For these reasons, it has been used for centuries as a dressing for wounds, including during World War I. Interestingly, though, along with hay and roses, it can also carry a fungus, *Sporothrix schenckii*. This fungus can cause an infection known as sporotrichosis, sometimes referred to as rose gardener's disease. Most commonly it infects the skin, entering through cuts and abrasions. As a protective measure, I think it's wise to use disposable gloves when working with sphagnum moss. It's also best to wet it before handling it too much to keep the dust down.

Sphagnum peat moss, often simply called peat moss, is a very common soil amendment and a major component of soilless potting mixes. Peat moss is not at all a sustainable crop. Nature cannot regenerate a peat bog at anywhere near the rate at which we are using peat moss. For this reason, we should greatly reduce its use and substitute more renewable resources, such as compost and coir, while continuing to identify other products. The use of peat is not limited to horticulture—it is also used as fuel, among other things. The long-fiber sphagnum used in horticultural projects, such as the projects listed in this book, constitutes a much more limited use of sphagnum. Additionally, it is only the upper portions that are harvested, not the deeper, older layers.

Making Moss Baskets

Moss baskets are both visually and functionally soft, natural ways to hang plants. A variety of ferns are commonly sold as hanging baskets. However, these are typically growing in plastic containers. While some species are comfortable in plastic, many others that grow naturally up in the air will not thrive in plastic containers. Additionally, plastic nursery pots are not as decorative or interesting from an aesthetic standpoint. Moss baskets, however, can be created in a variety of appealing styles.

Keep your eyes open. Anything that has good open drainage and aeration with a sturdy framework can be used for a moss basket. Wire-frame baskets will essentially vanish under the moss, while a wooden framework usually remains more visible. Some more decorative styles are also available; they can combine a distinctive flare with this naturalistic form. Basket frames can be readily found in many shapes and sizes.

Moss baskets are versatile and don't have to be hung. They can also be beautifully displayed sitting on a table or shelf or raised up on a plant stand or pedestal.

The type of fern you select will determine the type of growing medium to use for this project. For example, epiphytic ferns do not naturally grow in soil and will require a medium closer to their natural environment, such as bark chips.

WHAT YOU'LL NEED

- I'm using a 10-inch (25 cm) wire basket. Some other options include wooden baskets and terracotta with open designs, available in assorted shapes and sizes.
- Hanger, if desired.
- Long-fiber sphagnum moss and a bowl of water for soaking.
- Well-drained fern potting mix, enough to fill the container at most.
- Four 4-inch (10 cm) potted ferns. The number of plants used and their pot sizes will be based on the size of your container.
- Scissors.

STEPS

1 | Completely wring out some sphagnum moss as you would a sponge. Starting at the bottom, begin to line the basket with moss. Make sure the pads of moss are thick enough, and that you overlap them to prevent the soil from falling through.

2 | Because I will be planting three of the ferns into the sides of this basket, I will stop mossing at the level that I want to insert the ferns. Planting into the sides will yield fuller and quicker coverage. The entire basket will be covered with their delicate fronds.

3 | Add some potting mix, staying below the moss line.

4 | Spread your pointer and middle fingers apart and place them over the top of the pot and around the base of the plant. Turn the pot over, and with your other hand, gently shake or tap the plant out of its pot. Gently loosen the rootball, remove a little soil, and compress it with your hands to make it fit through the grid of the basket more easily. Working from the outside, gently push the rootball through an opening in the grid.

5 | Repeat the process with the second fern, using an opening a third of the way around the basket. Repeat for the third fern, going another third of the way around the basket.

6 | Wring out more sphagnum moss, and continue lining the basket all the way up, going over the basket edge a little. Add more potting mix, stopping about ½ inch (13 mm) below the edge. With your fingers pointing straight down, firm the mix around the three rootballs. Next, use your hand to scoop out a hole in the center for the last fern.

7 | Prepare the last fern (but there's no need to compress it) and place it in the hole, making sure that the soil line of the rootball is even with the soil line in the basket (½ inch [13 mm] below the edge). Add soil as needed. Firm in around the rootball of the last plant and give the basket a little shake to smooth and even out the mix. Use scissors to trim the moss and make it neat. Attach the hanger to the basket.

The finished planting includes: *Davallia mariesii* var. *stenolepis*.

If you find that your moss baskets dry out too quickly, try this trick. After covering the bottom of the basket's interior with moss, take a shallow saucer, as wide as will fit, and place it in the bottom. Continue filling with mix and plant as usual. You could also use a piece of heavy-duty plastic to line the bottom, but make sure you poke some drainage holes into it first. You can also buy preformed liners, typically made of coir, for standard-sized baskets and just drop them in place. If you want to plant into the sides, cut an "X" into the liner with a sharp knife or scissors, and push the plant through the opening.

Constructing a Fern Mount

Mounts are sometimes referred to as slabs, plaques, or shingles. Many ferns grow happily when mounted to cork slabs, pieces of wood, or actual branches. These sculptural bases lend an architectural dimension to mounted plants. They are often the most natural-looking forms and are also the most natural way for these plants to grow.

Select epiphytic fern species that will feel at home with this method. Avoid ferns that grow in soil because they will generally dry out too fast, and therefore are not suitable for mounting. Depending on the species you choose, this type of planting may need very regular watering. Be prepared to water as much and as often as is needed. Plunge them into a bucket or give them a little shower and let them drip-dry in your bathroom.

Hang mounted ferns from the ceiling or a wall, singly or in clusters, or simply rest them on a table. Mounts are the perfect way to explore your design prowess and be creative. Mounted displays are anything but ordinary and suggest a feeling of the wild tropics.

WHAT YOU'LL NEED

- Tree round or "cookie," cork slab, or even a piece of plywood.
- Marking pen.
- Drill.
- Hammer and large nail.
- Paper-wrapped wire, plastic-coated wire, or monofilament fishing line. You could also use florist's wire or nylon string.
- Screw eyes or small nails with heads.
- Long-fiber sphagnum moss and a bowl of water for soaking.
- One 6-inch (15 cm) potted fern. The number of plants used and their pot sizes will be based on the piece you are mounting on.
- Wire cutters.

STEPS

1 | Look at your tree round and decide what you want to be the top and the front, and where you want to hang the piece from. Mark the location for the hanger.

2 | For wood pieces, it is usually easiest to drill the hole. However, you can take a hammer and drive a large nail through the piece if necessary. Always use care with power tools. Drill a hole all the way through, making sure to hold the wood firmly in place, and not to drill through the table.

3 | Put the plastic-coated wire through the hole. Determine how much you want and cut it with the wire cutters. Cross the two ends, leaving at least 1 inch (2.5 cm) on each side, and twist the two together a couple of turns. Then, take one tail and twist it back down on itself tightly, and do the same with the other tail. This is your hanging loop.

4 | Spread your pointer and middle fingers apart and place them over the top of the pot and around the base of the plant. Turn the pot over, and with your other hand gently shake or tap the plant out of its pot. Gently loosen the rootball and remove some soil, exposing some of the roots without damaging them.

5 | Decide the placement and orientation of your fern on the wood. Use your pen to mark the outer edge of the rootball onto the tree round.

6 | Remove the fern, then hammer in some nails around where you made your mark. The nails serve as anchors for your wire.

7 | Completely wring out some sphagnum moss, as you would a sponge. Make a moss pad in the place you've chosen to place your fern.

8 | Cut a piece of paper-coated wire about 6 feet (1.8 m) long. Attach one end of the wire to one of the nails and twist it tightly.

9 | Place the rootball on top of the sphagnum moss. Begin to crisscross the wire, securing the rootball. Wrap it tightly around the nails as you go back and forth.

10 | Once you've basically secured it, twist it tight a few rounds, and leave the long tail in place.

11 | Wring out more moss, and pack it all over and around the rootball. Take the tail and, again, begin crisscrossing over and around the mossed rootball. When it is fully secured, twist it around one of the nails, and then twist it around some of the other wire tightly. Trim it if there's a lot of excess.

The finished project includes:
Platycerium bifurcatum.

10

 FABULOUS CORK

Cork is the outer bark of the cork oak tree, *Quercus suber*. It is native to the Mediterranean region, where it makes up a forest ecosystem. Cork's usage dates back as far as 3000 BCE, when it was used to make corks and to seal vessels. Much of the harvest comes from Portugal, where people have been harvesting cork for 300 years. It is still harvested by hand, a skill passed down through generations.

The cork oak is the only tree that can have its bark removed without killing it. It's harvested every nine years, and the trees have an average lifespan of 200 years. This is a very sustainable practice that keeps the ecosystem going. Cork is naturally waterproof, biodegradable, nontoxic, and totally renewable, making it the perfect base for your mounts!

11

Cork also makes a wonderful mount. Here are two *Asplenium antiquum* 'Leslie' on a cork piece.

In addition, a simple painted slab of plywood is another option for mounting ferns. Shown here is *Microsorum musifolium* 'Crocodyllus'.

Fashioning a Moss Pole

Moss poles offer another naturalistic way to grow and display your ferns. Structurally, moss poles are formed from wire mesh rolled into a column, stuffed with moss, and planted, much the same way many topiary forms are made. You can get even more creative and make different shapes. Moss poles can be small and delicate or large and robust. They can be planted with a single fern species, in a pattern using several species, or in an informal design.

Epiphytic ferns are perfectly suited to this style. Some soil-dwelling ferns might be able to adapt to this style, too, as long as you have enough of a moss base or other medium to hold enough water.

This type of planting usually requires very regular watering. Make sure you are prepared to water as much and as often as is needed. Plunge them into a bucket or give them a little shower and let them drip-dry in your bathroom. If you use several different fern species, they should be compatible with each other in terms of the care and conditions they require. Keep in mind that the top of the column will likely dry out faster than the bottom. Take advantage of this and put ferns that are tolerant of less moisture at the top, and those that need the most moisture at the

bottom. See the sidebar at the end of this project for a great way to build an internal irrigation system for larger moss poles.

For a fun display, suspend your moss pole from the ceiling or a wall hook. For more variety, try standing one up in a pot. You can even include them in a terrarium. It's easy and fun to make your own collection of moss poles.

WHAT YOU'LL NEED

- A piece of chicken wire. If you plan to make a larger column, use a heavier wire grid mesh that can hold its own shape and the extra weight. These types of grids also offer bigger planting "holes," so you can usually use 4-inch (10 cm) pots.
- Measuring tape.
- Wire cutters.
- Long-fiber sphagnum moss and a bowl of water for soaking.
- If you are making a larger column and plan to add some potting mix, have some well-drained fern potting mix available.
- Twelve 2-inch (5 cm) potted ferns. The number of plants used and their pot sizes will be based on the size of your column.

- Chopsticks or similar-sized stakes.
- Scissors.
- Plastic-coated wire or a ready-made hanger, if desired.

STEPS

1 | Have your design planned out ahead of time. Measure the chicken wire to the desired size. Make sure you allow for an extra row of your grid along the length and at the bottom. These will be needed to secure the column. Use wire cutters to cut to size. Keep the wire pegs on one long side.

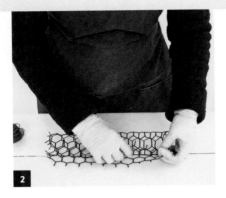
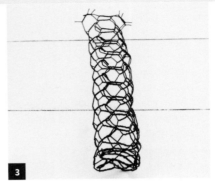

2 | Roll up the chicken wire, leaving the wire pegs at the end. Once rolled, it's time to secure it. Fold the wire pegs over the grid underneath, one at a time, and bend them back to "hook" the mesh closed.

3 | Choose the end with the stronger pegs and close the bottom. Leave the top open.

4 | Completely wring out some sphagnum moss as you would a sponge. Stuff some of the moss into the bottom of the column. This column is 2 inches (5 cm) wide and 10 inches (25 cm) high.

5 | Start planting from the bottom. Take a plant out of its pot and loosen the rootball, removing some of the soil and exposing the roots. Gently squeeze the rootball and push it through the opening in the grid. You can rock it back and forth as you push it in and stretch the grid open a little. Note: If your mesh is too small to fit the rootball through, you can clip the mesh (as little as possible!), put your plant through the hole, and then wire the hole back closed again to keep the plant in place. Make sure the soil line is just behind the wire grid—if you bury the plant it will rot.

6 | Prepare the next fern as you did the first and put it in place. I've chosen four plants each of three types and am planting them in a spiral fashion at even intervals. Wring out more moss, and continue stuffing the column as you go, alternating between a piece of moss and a plant. If you can't fit your fingers in, use the chopstick to tuck moss into all the open spaces. You don't want your roots to dry out.

7 | If necessary, stick the chopstick right down the center of the column to help position the rootballs.

8 | Continue planting and filling with moss. You can add a final plant at the top, or not. Either way, when you are done planting, fold your wire pegs over to close off the top securely.

9 | If you intend to hang it, use a ready-made hanger or decide how big a loop you want. Cut a piece of strong, flexible coated wire, big enough to cross over the top. Make as big a loop as you want and leave at least an extra 1 inch (2.5 cm) on either end. Put one end through the second row of the grid and, taking at least 1 inch (2.5 cm) for a tail, fold it back on itself and twist it tightly all the way up.

10 | Put the other end through the second row of the grid on the opposite side. Keeping your loop the size you want, take at least 1 inch (2.5 cm) for the tail, fold it back on itself, and twist it tightly all the way up. Trim any excess. Now it's ready for hanging.

The finished planting includes: *Asplenium antiquum* 'Osaka', *Nephrolepis cordifolia* 'Lemon Buttons', and *Pteris cretica* 'Mayii'.

Variations for Moss Poles

Instead of hanging your moss pole, you can stand it up in a decorative pot. When it's all planted, insert a chopstick, bamboo stake, or metal rod into the bottom of the pole, going up the center. Insert it at least halfway up. The heavier your pole, the stronger your stick needs to be, and the farther up your stick should be inserted. Make sure that enough of the stick remains for it to reach the bottom of the container you will be using.

Place your pole with the stick in the center of a decorative pot and hold it upright, with the stick resting on the bottom of the pot. Fill in with small pebbles, all around, bringing it up to just cover the base of the moss pole and leaving a ¼-inch (6 mm) lip below your pot rim. Your moss pole should be secure. Pebbles or rocks make great filler; you want to give the pot a lot of weight so it doesn't topple over. You could also put some heavy rocks or weights in the bottom of the pot, and if these provide enough ballast, you can fill the rest with whatever you like. Make sure your container has a drainage hole so that excess water can escape.

The finished planting includes: *Asplenium antiquum*, *Pteris nipponica*, *Polystichum tsussimense*, and *Nephrolepis exaltata* 'Emina'.

Another variation is to plant your moss pole horizontally, as if it were a log. This can be very handsome! Suspend it from both ends or set it in a long dish. Try your hand at decorative seasonal and holiday plantings, using premade wire forms, such as wreaths, spheres, or trees, or create your own. Fill with moss, and soil if desired, and plant a living wreath for the tabletop or to hang. Ferns display the most beautiful greens, and it's nice to have greenery that is alive and growing! Add decorative touches as you please.

If you are making thicker moss poles, it becomes increasingly harder to soak the medium within. One helpful trick is to cut a piece of PVC pipe the length of your column. Then drill holes all over the pipe, from the top to the very bottom, every few inches. For a narrow column, use a narrower piece of PVC. For a wider column, use PVC with a wider diameter. Seal off the bottom of the pipe with a pipe cap and place this tube in the center of your column as you are building it. Pack your potting medium and/or moss around it. When it's time to water, water the outside and fill up the tube. It will drain out through the holes and water the medium from within.

Creating Fern Prints

Fern prints use living green plants to make art. By pounding on the leaves, you transfer the plant's image onto fabric or paper. These highly desirable, ornamental prints are basically controlled chlorophyll stains—or grown up, glorified grass stains! Make prints on clothing and linens such as towels, tablecloths, and napkins; fabric for various decorative uses; and paper for frame-worthy artwork. They are simply beautiful on their own, but you can easily embellish them further if you desire. Paint them with touches of color, or stitch on some color and texture with additional needlework or beading.

To make a fern print, you'll need to use a very heavy hammer, which makes this a good way to get in a little exercise. And if you've had a bad day, it's a great way to release your tension. You will need a very sturdy surface to work on—such as a basement floor—and should also realize that the process will be very noisy for a few minutes.

Fern prints are very versatile, and every creation is completely unique. Fern printing is a personal favorite of mine.

WHAT YOU'LL NEED

- Heavy wood board (to protect the floor).
- Large, thin sheet of cardboard.
- Canvas fabric or linen napkin for printing.
- Heavy-duty tape. (I chose white duct tape to match the fabric color.)
- Large, sturdy sheet of paper. I use the paper from a large sketch pad.
- Fresh fern fronds.
- Framed canvas.
- Scissors.
- Pencil.
- Heavy lump hammer.

STEPS

1 | Tape the cardboard onto the wooden board. The cardboard provides a smooth surface under the fabric.

2 | Place the area of the linen that you will be printing on the cardboard. Plan your design first. I want to print on the corner of this napkin, so it will be visible even when it's folded. Note: If there are folds or wrinkles in the areas you want to print on, iron them first to smooth the fabric. Put the fern between two pieces of paper towel and blot off all moisture.

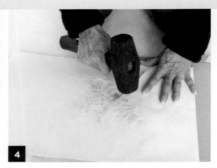

3 | Place your fern where and as you want it. Cover the fern with sturdy, white paper, being careful not to move it. Move the board onto the floor or other suitable surface.

4 | Holding the paper and fabric firmly in place, begin pounding the paper over the fern. Hold the paper as close as possible to the area that you're pounding and be very careful not to hit yourself. If the fern, paper, or fabric shifts, it will blur your design. You might want to practice one first. Pound as hard as you can repeatedly in one spot before continuing along. Work in one direction, moving from one end to the other.

5 | Once you have completely pounded the whole fern, very gently and slowly begin to peel back the paper. If the design didn't transfer, you may need to cover it up again and pound some more.

6 | See the print on the napkin and on the paper! The paper is beautiful in its own right and could be framed as art as well.

TO MAKE A HANGING CANVAS

1 | Place the framed canvas on the canvas fabric to be printed. Be sure to have the right side of the fabric facing up. Measure out how much you will need to cover the entire front and a border all the way around that you will tape in back when done. Cut your fabric to size.

2 | With the frame still centered on the canvas fabric, pencil a line all the way around to mark the boundary for your design. Now, take the fabric, create your design with some fronds (working within the pencil-line boundary), and make your print following the steps outlined on the previous page.

3 | Line the printed fabric up on the frame.

4 | Fold one edge over and tape the corners in back. Repeat on the opposite edge.

5 | Cover your work surface with clean paper or toweling and place the print face down. Tape the entire length of both edges. This keeps the print flat and secure and prevents the fabric from fraying. It also looks nicer.

6 | Now fold in the remaining edges and wrap it like a present. To make it less bulky, cut the little flap of fabric on top where it meets the tape at the edge of the frame, and remove it. Tape the entire length to the edge of the frame.

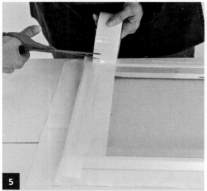

Making Pressed Fern Art

Botanists have been pressing plants since the 1500s. By collecting pieces of plants, pressing them flat, and drying them, you can preserve them. Mounted on paper and intended for study, these botanical specimens are often quite attractive. Their beauty didn't go unnoticed in Victorian England. It was quite fashionable for ladies to collect and press plants in order to create picturesque albums for viewing pleasure. Today, the pressing technique is basically unchanged, and creating artistic specimens for decoration is increasingly popular.

Although dried and pressed ferns may no longer be alive, they are still the real deal and lend a truly naturalistic element to artwork. Make pictures for hanging, create notecards, or start a keepsake album. Their look complements any style of décor. If you like the idea of working with pressed plants but want even more creative freedom, try a variation of this theme: clipped pressed art. Instead of using your dried pressed specimens in whole pieces, you can clip them into smaller segments and recombine the pieces to create all kinds of artful designs.

You can make pressed art of any size. It is a quick, easy, inexpensive decorating fix, and it makes a great gift, too!

WHAT YOU'LL NEED

- Pruning shears.
- Fern fronds.
- Paper towels.
- Several sheets of newspaper.
- A big, heavy book. You can also buy or make your own plant press.
- Sturdy paper for your finished design.
- Mat for framing, if desired.
- Frame.
- Ruler.
- Pencil.
- Scissors.
- Scrap paper for working on.
- Flat knife.
- White glue.
- Pointed toothpicks.
- Paper towel or napkin.
- Heavy washers for weights.

STEPS

1 | Harvest your fronds using pruning shears. Place your fronds between paper towels, and blot completely dry. Place dried fronds on one side of the newspaper, fold over, and cover with the other side. Place a heavy book on top. Let the fronds press and dry for a minimum of 24 hours—I often wait a week.

2 | Measure and cut your final mounting paper to fit inside the frame. If using a mat, cut the paper to the outside dimensions of the mat. Trim away any excess.

3

4

3 | Mark the inside of the mat (or the frame if you're not using a mat) so you know the boundary for your design.

4 | Carefully remove the dried specimens from the newspaper and create your design. You might want to play with it on a piece of scrap paper first, so as not to ruin your mounting sheet. When you're ready, use a pencil to lightly mark the placement of your fronds.

5 | Slide the knife gently under the first frond and lift it up (for a complex design, start with the biggest frond first). Carefully turn it over onto a piece of scrap paper. Gently apply the tiniest drops of glue. You might want to practice some of these techniques before you do your final design.

6 | Use a toothpick to spread the glue even thinner. Then, use the knife to lift the frond from the paper.

7 | Gently turn the frond over, taking care not to touch the glue. Place the bottom on its mark and hold gently with one finger. Pivot the top of the frond over to its mark and put it in place.

8 | Place a paper towel over the frond and press down gently but firmly. If necessary, wrap a napkin tightly around your pointer finger and carefully dab up any excess glue from the paper.

9 | Place weights all over the frond to hold it in place while the glue dries.

10 | It should be dry in a day. Once it's dry, carefully remove the weights. Remove the back from the frame, place the mat inside if you're using one, place your pressed art inside, and close the frame. Your artwork is ready for display.

Instead of mounting your pressed ferns in a permanent display, simply place them temporarily on a desk blotter, paper, or even fabric. Splatter or brush paint all over and around them to create cool fern silhouettes. Another option is to find a recipe for making your own paper, and then for added beauty and interest, add bits of fern leaves to the mix.

Clipped Pressed Art

Create clipped art using all the techniques described above. Take your dried fronds and clip them into smaller pieces. Assemble them, creating your own unique design.

Making Cyanotypes

A cyanotype, one of the oldest "photographic" techniques, is a photochemical blueprinting. It was first discovered in 1842 by Sir John Herschel, an English scientist, who used the method mainly to produce copies of diagrams. These were the original blueprints.

The process is based on a chemical's sensitivity to ultraviolet light. After a piece of paper or fabric is coated with a solution of the chemical, it is then exposed to sunlight, which includes ultraviolet light. The light reacts with the chemical, and a complex chemical reaction follows, resulting in an insoluble blue dye called Prussian blue. Any part of the paper or fabric that is covered before being exposed to the light will remain white (or whatever the original color of the paper or fabric was). Any part that is exposed turns blue.

Anna Atkins (1799–1871) was an English botanist and is often considered the first female photographer. She is very well known for her work with cyanotypes. Anna used this process to document plant life, most notably ferns, algae, and seaweed. After treating the paper with the chemical solution, she would place the specimens directly onto the coated paper and expose it to sunlight. She produced a series of impressive

books filled with these blue Victorian photograms.

Nowadays you might hear of cyanotypes being called sunprints. A variety of kits and a wide assortment of pretreated paper and fabric in many colors are readily available. If you are more adventurous, you can still obtain the same chemicals and treat your own paper or fabric. Make clothing, linens, decorative artwork for display, notecards, and much more. This is an easy and exciting project for children, and fun for the whole family.

WHAT YOU'LL NEED

- Paper towels.
- Fern fronds.
- Plain scrap paper.
- A sturdy, lightweight board. I use foam board.
- Pretreated papers and/or napkins in lightproof bags.
- Heavy black paper, cloth, or plastic.
- Plexiglas or glass sheet.
- Sturdy, flat piece of corrugated cardboard.
- A sunny day.
- A sink or bathtub for rinsing.

STEPS

1 | Blot the fern fronds dry with paper towels. Do a mock-up of your designs on plain paper. Ready everything you plan to make in advance. You cannot expose the treated materials to light for very long. Try to avoid working in a sunny, bright room. Because the fern fronds are only creating a silhouette here, they don't have to be fresh and green. If you press them for a day or so, it will make them nice and flat and easy to work with, and they will create sharper images.

2 | If you are doing more than one cyano-type project at a time, place them on your foam board to make sure they will all fit.

3 | Have the lightproof bags with pretreated materials on hand. Remove the treated paper from the bag and swap it out for the plain paper. This notecard is actually light blue paper but looks dark blue because of the chemical coating.

1

4 | Immediately cover with the lightproof package to block out light. You can also use heavy, black paper for covering.

5 | Remove the next piece of treated paper from its bag and swap it out for the plain paper. Be careful not to mess up your design. This sheet is white paper but looks blue due to the chemical coating. Transfer your design to the treated sheet. When done, immediately cover with the lightproof package to block out light.

6 | If you're making a napkin instead of paper, remove the treated napkin from its bag and open it completely on the foam board. Place your design. This napkin is white but appears blue due to the chemical coating.

7 | As soon as the last piece is ready, carefully remove the black pouches and cover the entire board with a sheet of plexiglas (glass works perfectly, too). Set it down carefully so as not to move any of the fronds. Take care not to get smudges on the plexiglas.

8 | Immediately cover with a piece of heavy, black paper. A heavy, black cloth or thick black plastic will also work.

9 | Carefully place the foam board onto a piece of corrugated cardboard. This makes it easier to move around. Carry it outside and place it in a flat spot in direct sunlight. From noon to early afternoon is the best time of day. Remove the black paper and leave it in the sun for 20 to 30 minutes. Stay with it to make sure that nothing disturbs it or falls on it. Remove anything that lands on the plexiglas, and make sure no shadows fall on it.

10 | Bring everything inside exactly as it is. At this point, you have only printed one side of your pieces. If you want to print on both sides, a napkin for example, turn the piece over and repeat the entire process right away. Even if you don't want to make a design, the backside of the piece will ultimately be the original color. For example, the napkin will be white on the back. If you want it to be the same blue as the front, you must expose the back to sunlight for the same amount of time. When you are done exposing your pieces, begin rinsing them in the sink, one at a time. Handle paper gently and try not to rub it.

11 | Notice the transformation of the coloring! When you are finished rinsing, lay the paper flat to dry.

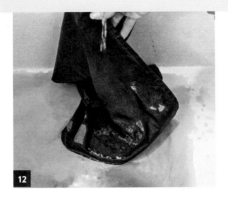

12 | For the napkin, run it under water, watching all the chemicals rinsing out.

13 | When you are done rinsing the napkin, wring the excess water out of the fabric, shake it out, and lay it flat to dry.

14 | The dark blue napkin was exposed to 30 minutes of strong midday sun, hence the strong coloration. The medium blue napkin didn't get any direct sun, and it was at the very end of the day. The less you expose your item to sunlight, the lighter blue it will be. You decide.

Nephrolepis cordifolia 'Lemon Button'

By buying papers treated with different colors, you can create beautiful, colored notecards or fun pieces to frame.

ABOUT THE AUTHOR

MOBEE WEINSTEIN is the foreman of gardeners for outdoor gardens at the New York Botanical Garden (NYBG) in the Bronx. She has a degree in plant studies and has done postgraduate work in botany. She taught indoor plants as an adjunct professor at the State University of New York (SUNY) and is a regular instructor at the New York Botanical Garden. She has appeared representing the NYBG on television (NBC, ABC, *Martha Stewart Living*, and others) and radio (Ralph Snodsmith's *The Garden Hotline* program and more). She is a frequent lecturer to outside organizations and a judge for the Philadelphia Flower Show (ferns and other plant classes). She has also judged the NYC Community Gardens and organized and led field trips for the NYBG School of Professional Horticulture. She has published more than a dozen articles and book chapters on various topics, including ferns and water lilies.

PHOTO CREDITS

❧ INDEX ❧

R

Repotting, 48, 49
Resurrection ferns, 28
Rhizomes, 23, 26
Ribbon fern, 76
Rita's Gold Boston fern, 64
Roots (fern), 23, 24
Rough maidenhair fern, 51
Royal fern, 110
Rumohra adiantiformis, 78

S

Sandy soil, 84
Saucer terrarium, 128
Scott's spleenwort (Dragontail fern), 93
Scouring rush, 15, 105
Seed plants, 12–15, 19, 21
Seedless plants, 10, 12
Selagine ella kraussiana 'Aurea,' 124
Selaginella braunii, 116
Selaginella erythropus, 128
Selaginella kraussiana 'Aurea,' 1124
Selaginella uncinata, 128
Sensitive fern, 109
Sexual propagation, 29–30
Sickle fern, 66
Silhouettes, fern, 178
Silica, 15, 105
Silver lace fern, 74
Soil, for outdoor ferns, 84–85
Soilless mixes, 38
Southern maidenhair fern, 52
Spanish moss, 130, 138
Sphaeropteris cooperi (syn. Cyathea cooperi), 79
Sphagnum moss, 128, 141, 142, 151, 153, 154, 157, 158, 163, 164
Spider brake fern, 75
Sporangia, 22, 32, 33
Spores, 12, 22, 29–30
Sporophyte, 30, 31, 33
Spring, fern care in, 88

Squirrel's foot fern, 59
Staghorn fern, 36, 71
Stems (fern), 26
Stipe (fern), 23, 25
Sunprints (cyanotypes), 179–185
Sweet root fern (Licorice fern), 112
Sword brake fern (Silver lace fern), 74
Synthetic (inorganic) fertilizers, 46

T

Tabletop garden, 137–139
Temperature(s), 37, 81, 87
Terrariums, 120–128
Terrestrial ferns, 27
Thelypteris noveboracensis (syn. *Parathelypteris noveboracensis*), 117
Tongue fern, 77
Transplanting ferns, 48–50
Tsus-sima holly fern, 36
Tuber sword fern, 63

V

Vascular plants, 10, 11–12, 19–20, 22. *See also* Ferns
Vertical garden, 129–133

W

Watering
  indoor ferns, 40–43
  moss pole, 162
  outdoor ferns, 87
  terrariums, 126
Weeds, 48
Western Sword Fern, 115
Whitei, 60

X

Xeric ferns, 27, 28

Y

Yellow leaves, 48